*Running an Effective
Sales Office*

*Other titles from Marketing Improvements Limited*

Managing a Sales Force

Training Salesmen on the Job

Recruiting and Selecting
  Successful Salesmen

Negotiating Profitable Sales

Motivating Your Sales Force

How to Handle Major Customers
  Profitably

The Management of Marketing

# Running an Effective Sales Office

**PATRICK FORSYTH**
**of Marketing Improvements Limited**

**Gower**

©Marketing Improvements Limited 1980

Published by Gower Publishing Company Limited
Westmead, Farnborough, Hants, England

Forsyth, Patrick
 Running an effective sales office.
 1. Sales management
 1. Title
651'.32     HF548

 ISBN 0-566-02185-4

Printed in Great Britain by Biddles Limited, Guildford, Surrey

# Contents

List of illustrations                                                                vii

Preface                                                                              ix

Acknowledgements                                                                     xi

**PART I    The Sales Office and the Marketing Operation**                           1
   1   What is Marketing?                                             3
   2   The Role of the Sales Office                                   8

**PART II   Managing and Controlling Sales Office Activity**                        17
   3   Setting up the Organisation                                   19
   4   Managing Time                                                 30
   5   Managing Systems                                              34
   6   Controlling                                                   39

**PART III  Increasing Sales**                                                      51
   7   The Sales Approach                                            53
   8   Company Image                                                 61
   9   Response Activities                                           71
  10   Initiated Activities                                              92
  11   Support Activities                                                96
  Appendix 1   Telephone Selling                                         103

**PART IV   Maintaining an Effective Inside Sales Team**                           107
  12   Development and Appraisal                                         109
  13   Delegation                                                        115
  14   Motivation                                                        119
  Appendix 2   Leadership                                                128

SUMMARY: Keys to Success                                                           132

Further Reading                                                                    138

Index                                                                              140

# Contents

List of Illustrations

Acknowledgements

PART I   The Sales Office and the Marketing Function
1   What is Marketing?
2   The Role of the Sales Office

PART II   Managing and Controlling Sales Office Activity
3   Structuring the Organisation
4   Manpower Plans
5   Managing Systems
6   Controlling

PART III   Increasing Sales
7   The Sales Approach
8   Company Image
9   Response Activities
10   Inbound Activities
11   Outbound Activities
Appendix 1   Telephone Selling

PART IV   Sharpening an Effective Inside Sales Team
12   Recruitment and Appraisal
13   Training
14   Motivation
Appendix 2   Leadership

SEMINAR 1   Sales Courses

Further Reading

Index

# Illustrations

2.1    Sales office: communication links    9

2.2    The sales office: position in company hierarchy    10

2.3    Progress towards a decision to buy    14

2.4    Sales office influence on progress towards a decision to buy    14

3.1    The nature of sales office activity    19

3.2    The sequence of sales office activity    21

3.3    Operating manual: departmental objectives, activities and ✓ responsibilities    23

3.4    Operating manual: contact chart    24

3.5    Operating manual: job descriptions    25

3.6    Operating manual: operating procedures    26

3.7    Operating manual: operating procedures/demonstration by specimen form    27

3.8    Operating manual: operating procedures/graphic demonstration in network analysis style    28

4.1    Scheduling backwards to meet deadlines    31

4.2    Planning our time    32

5.1    A technological scenario    35

5.2    Checking for duplicated information    36

6.1    Creative visual presentation of figures — a discount calculator for salesmen    45

6.2a    Bar chart showing how some representatives have been found to spend an average 7-hour day    46

6.2b    Bar chart showing half-year comparison of representatives' progress towards targets    46

6.3    Pie chart comparing customer mix (by order volume) of customer selling 'gift' product    47

| | | |
|---|---|---|
| 6.4 | Presenting information from figures: histogram | 47–8 |
| 6.5 | Time chart showing seasonal fluctuations | 48 |
| 7.1 | The buying sequence | 54 |
| 7.2 | Differing viewpoints of salesman/customer | 56 |
| 7.3 | Product feature/benefit analysis | 58 |
| 7.4 | Subjective/objective reasons for buying | 59 |
| 7.5 | Four sources of benefits | 60 |
| 8.1 | Checkpoints for satisfactory letters | 68 |
| 8.2 | Examining time factors from the customer's viewpoint | 69 |
| 9.1 | Example of enquiry progress form | 73 |
| 9.2 | Example of complaint form | 75 |
| 9.3 | Poor complaint-handling letter | 78 |
| 9.4 | Good complaint-handling letter | 79 |
| 9.5 | Sales letters: reading sequence | 82 |
| 9.6 | Sales letters: use of language | 84 |
| 9.7 | Structuring and directing a telephone call towards our objective | 88 |
| 10.1 | Generating ongoing turnover from the sales office | 94 |
| 11.1 | Selecting the course of an enquiry | 101 |
| 12.1 | The continuous cycle of development | 110 |
| 12.2 | Example of assessment form | 111 |
| 14.1 | Herzberg's satisfiers and dissatisfiers | 121 |
| 14.2 | Time relationship of impacts on motivational balance | 126 |
| 14.3 | The ideal/real manager | 126 |
| A.1 | Interaction of areas in effective leadership | 128 |
| S.1 | Ten-step decision-making | 135 |
| S.2 | Knowledge and skills checklist | 137 |

# *Preface*

The main objective of this book is to help managers and supervisors in the difficult task of planning, organising and controlling the sales office operation with maximum effectiveness. That is, to ensure that it carries on the necessary administrative activities in a way which supports its main aim, that of making, or helping ultimately to make, sales.

The book recognises throughout that a 'sales conscious' attitude to every aspect of the activity can contribute to more sales being made either now or in the future. The 'sales office' may be regarded by some as a backwater of activity, but it is one that can, and does in many oganisations, make a major contribution to effectiveness and business results.

The book sets out to review the many interrelated areas of activity, skill and knowledge required in running all or part of any 'inside' sales section effectively. In so doing, it provides a means of briefing for new situations, and reviewing those already occurring.

It sets out to help the reader to acquire practical ideas on improving routines and increasing sales. Sales improvement is in turn dependent on the manager's knowing how to increase the sales awareness and selling performance of his or her office staff — the 'inside sales team' — and this too is covered in the book. None of this is possible, however, without an understanding of the context in which the section must operate and of how the sales office contributes directly to the company's total marketing operation. This requires an appreciation of what marketing is about — which is the starting point of the book.

It may be read through from beginning to end, or dipped into occasionally. The breakdown into chapters and subheadings also allows individual sections to be referred to or read at random.

As the area discussed relates so closely to the whole sales and marketing activity of the company, staff and managers in overlapping areas of activity — for example, the sales manager — may benefit from it as well as sales office managers, supervisors, section heads and those that come more immediately to mind.

Patrick Forsyth

Marketing Improvements Limited
Ulster House
17 Ulster Terrace
Regent's Park
London NW1 4PJ

# Acknowledgements

'Plagiarisation is stealing from one person, research is stealing from many.' This book is pure research (and this quotation is stolen).

It began some time ago as an observation, or rather two observations: first, that the sales office is a curiously neglected area both in the view many companies take of it, and as evidenced by the lack of guidance in written, or any other, form available to those who manage or work in such a section; and second, that it is an area which, effectively run, makes a major contribution to the efficiency and sales success of an organisation. The book took shape first as material for one of Marketing Improvements Ltd's range of public seminars, built up from observation and experience of many sales office situations and contributed to by the breadth of knowledge gained in MI's consultancy work. From the feedback from delegates and the addition of more recent experience, in Marketing Improvements' own business, in companies in a variety of industries and countries, the seminar has been progressively revised, updated and, I hope, improved. At one stage it was listed in Management Courses Index (now the National Training Index) 'High Spots'.

From this and other material this book has been 'assembled'. Thanks are due to a number of people. To David Collischon, a good friend throughout my business life, much of whose original thinking appears herein. To my colleagues at Marketing Improvements: David Senton, with whom I have perhaps worked most closely in my 10 years with Marketing Improvements, and who has always encouraged me towards new challenges; Peter Kirkby, who 'made' me run the course; and Mike Wilson, who formed Marketing Improvements, and John Lidstone, whose own writing has 'encouraged the others', both of whom play a crucial part in maintaining the company as a place where good and original work is possible, and new experience constantly developed. To my colleagues who have also conducted the seminar, and the delegates who have attended in the past, all of whom helped build up the information. Last, but by no means least, my thanks to Alan Reid, without whose journalistic skill and advice pen would never have been put to paper, and to Barbara Wright, who finally goaded both me and her typewriter to an extent that ensured completion.

There are many skills and techniques needed in managing or participating in the activity of a 'sales office' successfully. I hope that sufficient of this broad area of experience is touched upon here to stimulate those who seek to improve their own particular operation at least in some measure.

P.F.

# Part One

# The Sales Office and the Marketing Operation

# 1: *What is Marketing?*

Work in a typical sales office is characterised by its pace, volume and diversity. Those employed in one, or indeed managing one, need to be efficient, organised, tactful and persuasive — with the ability to handle three things at once, all of which relate to different areas of the business and all of which were wanted yesterday.

The danger is that within the sales office the battle between the urgent and the important is never won. The administrative area can submerge all else and the important is either not done or not done properly. The opportunity is that the sales office, if well set up and operating effectively, can not only make a major contribution to an organisation's sales results but can provide — for some customers — the prime reason for dealing with a particular supplier. It can in fact be a powerful element in many a company's marketing operation.

### The nature of marketing

'Marketing' has become one of the most popular words in business, but it is frequently misused and seldom explained to people who work in companies. It is a relatively new term — one which has evolved through business becoming increasingly complex.

Many wrongly use marketing as another word for selling, and others use it as a more impressive title for advertising. Marketing is concerned with selling, and with advertising, but it is much more.

Its place and purpose may not be immediately obvious, as finance or production are, mainly because it covers so many facets of business activity. It is easier to appreciate its function if we consider an old one-man craft business, such as village blacksmith or cabinet-maker. Such a man could easily see his working life as being made up of two major activities — making and selling. Because he knew his customers (the 'market' for his goods and services) as well as he knew his product, he would know whether he could supply or make it, and for how much; he could suggest products to customers; and he would not spend hours making a new product if he was not certain that he could sell it, and sell it for a price that made it all worth while.

When the one-man cabinet-maker becomes a big company, that once instinctive feeling for customer consideration and awareness has to be organised. 'Marketing' covers all the

3

arrangements and activities that go on to keep this combination of customer satisfaction, saleability and profitability co-ordinated and alive.

The Institute of Marketing defines marketing as:

> The management process responsible for identifying, anticipating and satisfying customer requirements profitably.

Even more simply we can say that marketing is 'Looking at the business through the customer's eyes and supplying value and satisfaction at a profit'. The combination of activities and interests which makes it so much more than simply selling, or advertising, is also well shown in another definition: 'Marketing is profitably supplying goods that don't come back, to customers that do.'

The 'market' consists of actual buyers (customers) and potential buyers. Market research means trying to discover how many customers (real and potential) there are, where they live, what their likes and dislikes are, how they buy, how much money they have and what they spend it on, what colours they like for a particular item, and so on, in order to make more accurate business decisions.

### The marketing system

Before looking at the position the sales office occupies in marketing, it is worth looking further at the marketing system. We have seen some simple explanations of what marketing sets out to do, but there are conflicts in this seemingly straightforward objective. For one thing, it is unusual for the aims of the company to be the same as the aims of its customers. The company would ideally like to sell its products for a very high profit, for instance, while the customers' main concern may be for the lowest possible price. Conflicts also arise within companies, and they must be reconciled. The different objectives of the design, accounting and sales departments, for instance, will put different interpretations on all sorts of daily problems.

It is one of the key functions of the marketing system to attempt to reconcile these conflicts or to find acceptable compromises. There are, therefore, four main elements in the marketing system, as follows:

1   The market and its segments.
2   The company and its functions.
3   The marketing mix.
4   The environment.

### The market and its segments

There is seldom a mass market for any product, though some companies presume that mass-marketing and advertising methods will successfully exploit such a mass market. Analysis has shown, however, that within each market there are actually a number of market segments, and this is true not only for common products which would be expected to have a 'mass market', such as breakfast cereals, butter, basic clothing; but also for more 'individual' products such as stereo equipment, cameras, jewellery, fashionable clothes; for industrial products such as components and equipment; and for services such as hotels or plant hire.

Each segment represents a group of actual or potential customers with the same need which can be satisfied with similar products. For example, within one market for cars there are segments interested particularly in economy, status, or carrying capacity etc.; and with detergents there are segments interested in softness (for the hands and clothes), cleaning power, economy etc. In industrial markets the same applies. Similar medical equipment sold to private clinics and to 'charity' hospitals in the Third World may perform the same function, but will have a different degree of sophistication for each segment. For a number of reasons (and quite often the effectiveness of a company's sales office is one of the factors) each segment of the market develops a degree of buyer loyalty which can range from total loyalty to total indifference. Instead of mass marketing, therefore, these segments often have to be tackled selectively and individually in order to achieve maximum profitability and the least conflict over the image of the company and its product.

### The company and its functions

Every company has three basic functions, though in a well-directed company they do not operate in isolation from each other, and two major resources. The three basic functions are

Production,
Finance, and
Marketing,

and the two major resources are

Capital, and
Labour.

Each function has different tasks and different objectives, often operates on a different time-scale, attracts different types of people, and regards money in a different way. So, despite their all contributing towards the same company objectives, there is inevitably internal conflict between, say, marketing and production, or production and finance. The Table 1.1, though to some extent a caricature, shows clearly how these conflicts and frictions occur. The sales office often finds itself 'pig in the middle' in some of these exchanges.

### The marketing mix

This describes 'the offering' of the company to the market, and consists of three elements: (a) the product range; (b) prices, discounts and terms; and (c) presentation, or means of communicating with the market (selling, sales promotion, advertising etc.). Juggling with these three elements enables a company to balance its objectives with the consumers' objectives.

The effect of technological development and the vigorous competition that exists in a capitalist society has resulted in products and prices of competing companies in most industries becoming increasingly similar. Consequently the first two elements of the marketing mix are becoming less important in customer choice, and presentation (the way in which the company tells the market about products and prices) has become crucial. Often it is the only differentiating element between companies.

Presentation inclues all communication techniques including advertising, promotion, direct mail, personal selling, merchandising, packaging and display etc. The sales office clearly has a role in the presentation area and thus provides, particularly through the vital element of service, one of the reasons for customers to make their choice between competitive offerings. Yet the feelings that the office would run so much better 'if it was not for all these customer demands' is still widespread amongst sales office personnel.

The three major functions of business and their differing goals and attitudes

| | Finance | Production | Marketing |
|---|---|---|---|
| Objective | To ensure that the return on capital employed will provide security, growth and yield | To optimise cost/output relationships | To maximise profitable sales in the market place |
| Time period of operation | Largely past — analysing results plus some forecasting | Largely present — keeping production going particularly in 3-shift working | Largely future — because of lead time in reacting to market place |
| Orientation | Largely inward — concerned with internal results of company | Largely inward — concerned with factory facilities for personnel | Largely outward — concerned with customers, distribution and competition |
| Attitudes to money | Largely 'debit and credit' — once money spent, it is gone, money not spent is saved | Largely 'cost effective — hence value analysis, value analysis techniques and cost cutting | Largely 'return on investment' — money 'invested' in promotion to provide 'return' in sales and profits |
| Personality | Often introverted; lengthy training; makes decisions on financially quantifiable grounds | Usually qualified in quantitative discipline; makes decisions on input/output basis | Often extroverted; often educationally unqualified; has to make some decisions totally qualitatively |

Table 1.1  How conflict arises between different company functions

*The environment*

This whole marketing system has to operate in an environment which restricts it. Such restrictions include:

1   Total demand.
2   Availability of capital and labour.
3   Competition (including international competition).
4   Legal requirements.
5   Supply of raw materials.
6   Channels of distribution — e.g. overseas agents and conditions

Any restrictions must be carefully considered, because of their effect on the business.

We can see then that marketing is vital to business survival, but that marketing is difficult to practise because of the conflicts within the company, and between the company and its customers. With prices and products becoming more and more similar, presentation grows increasingly important.

To carry out the marketing objective (identifying and satisfying customer requirements, at a profit) the company has a number of services to call on. While the sales force may be the 'front line' service, vital to the marketing effort, one of its main 'tactical weapons' and its principal support (without which it often could not function) is the sales office.

# 2: The Role of the Sales Office

Terms habitually used in a military sense have found acceptance in management as well. The function of marketing within a company (organising the company to meet consumer needs) is part of the company's 'strategy'; but if this broad concept is to be realised, 'tactical weapons' are required, operating on a more immediate basis.

The sales office is one of the 'tactical' weapons that the chief marketing executive can use to achieve his 'strategic' objectives. Its efficiency is absolutely critical to the success of the whole enterprise. Making and keeping it efficient requires a skill and judgement that is not always fully appreciated by the wielders of other, sometimes more glamorous, 'tactical weaponry' in a company.

A sales office can broadly be defined as *an internal operation within the sales structure, performing administrative and selling functions in support of the sales objectives.* A key word in this definition is 'support', but no one should ever associate support with secondary. To use military terms again, an army which is not supported by a supply of petrol, food, weapons and ammunitions is totally useless.

The definition also indicates that numerous activities are performed in the sales office. Depending on the size of the company and the volume of work, there may be separate departments for these activities; or specialist skills, the way the company operates or is located, and the nature of the market may require the functions of the sales office to be divided into sections. As often as not, however, they are all carried out by the same people, and are all managed simultaneously.

The fact that it is a support operation means that the majority of its jobs are 'reactive' — that is, they are done in response to a request or an action of some sort outside the department. But no successful department in any company goes long without initiating jobs as well; its staff would lose all enthusiasm if they never did anything unless it was in response to an instruction. There is a great deal of opportunity — far more than is often appreciated — for initiating action in a sales office.

The mixture of administrative and sales jobs, reactive and initiated, explains some of the problems commonly associated with running an effective sales office.

## *The sales office and the marketing cycle*

The work carried out by the sales office is all part of the company's general marketing operations, and we have already seen how marketing fits into the company as a whole. What are the marketing operations? Very simply, they can be seen as a cycle which starts with the customer establishing his needs, and is successfully completed when those needs are properly satisfied. The following are typical stages in the cycle:

THE CUSTOMER — has needs.

RESEARCH — establishes the precise nature of the needs, e.g. what sort of product or service is required, the extent of the market, the price at which the market will buy, when the product or service is required.

PRODUCT DEVELOPMENT — creates, develops and improves the product, ensuring that it continues to meet the consumer's (changing) needs.

SALES AND DISTRIBUTION — make the product or service readily available to the optimum number of consumers.

PROMOTION AND ADVERTISING — create the demand for the product, by persuasively informing the consumer and the distribution channels that the product or service exists, describing it and showing where/how it can be obtained.

THE CUSTOMER — has his needs satisfied.

The sales office has a unique position, for it is engaged in many, if not all, of these functions, and thus forms vital links between the company and its customers. In addition, it forms other vital links between various parts of the organisation (see example in Figure 2.1).

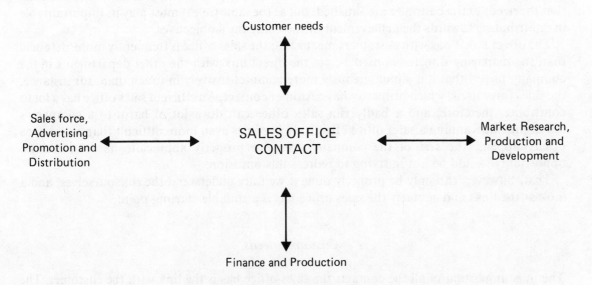

**Fig. 2.1 Sales office: communication links**

A specific version of such a chart can be used to describe and explain something of the role and relationship of a particular sales office to all its personnel. It will do so far more clearly than the sort of hierarchical organisation chart produced in many companies, where the sales office can appear low in order of importance (see Figure 2.2).

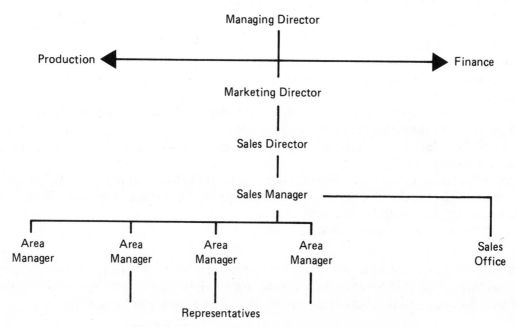

Fig. 2.2 **The sales office: position in company hierarchy**

The 'uniqueness' of the sales office's position ensures that there can be a good deal of interest and therefore enthusiasm in sales office work, but it also means that there is a difficult path to tread between conflicting requirements. The sales office performs a critical role in ensuring that the needs of the customer are satisfied, but at the same time it must play its important role in contributing towards the achievement of the company's objectives.

The direct link it has with customers means that the sales office is frequently more 'in touch' than the managing director himself is, yet the direct link with the other departments in the company means that it is simultaneously more comprehensively in touch than, for instance, the sales force itself, which primarily has customer contact. An efficient sales office has a lot to contribute, therefore, and a badly run sales office can do a lot of harm to a company's development. Running a sales office effectively becomes even more difficult than usual if, as often happens, the rest of the company does not properly appreciate its role, and no opportunity should be lost in trying to redress this omission.

That, however, can only be properly done if we fully understand the role ourselves, and a look at the links and contacts the sales office has is a suitable starting point.

### Customer needs

The most important of all the contacts the sales office has is the link with the customer. The sales office must always know what the customer wants, and the principal customer requirement is that the product should fulfil its claims. Good product knowledge is therefore essential, as well as good knowledge of advertising, packaging and promotional activity, for the sales office must be fully aware of what claims are being made for the product. It follows that complete confidence in the value of the product is necessary, and everyone must be able to give product information in the customer's terms.

Increasingly the customers' needs are becoming less exclusively associated with product features, and are taking service into account more and more. In a company that offers a service rather than a product, the 'secondary' or back-up service is growing to be an increasingly important customer need. In highly competitive industries there is frequently very little to distinguish one product from another. Obtaining an order, or building up 'product loyalty', can become dependent primarily on one factor — service. Service can gain or lose the initial order, and will then determine whether the customer places subsequent business.

There are countless opportunities for a customer to compare one company's service with another — availability of product, readiness with which information is supplied, speed of obtaining quotations, courtesy on the telephone, speed of handling an enquiry or a complaint. Every point of contact with a customer is an opportunity to illustrate the company's superiority. The focus on service also extends to internal service, a more suitable name than administration for some activities. An inefficient internal service means wrong delivery instructions, confusion over invoicing, incorrect statements, service contract renewals sent out late — petty irritations which make all the difference when the product itself had no significant advantage over a competitor's.

The sales office, often more than any other department, is vitally concerned with service. In this respect it has a dual role — service to the customer before, during and after fulfilment of the order, and service in support of the field force at all times. Further it must carry out this role with regard to the overall intentions operating within the company.

### Company needs — profit and growth

One of the basic aims of any company is to remain in business, and to do so it must be profitable — which means that revenue from sales must be higher than the total cost of getting them. Clearly the sales operation can directly and easily influence both turnover and cost, and everyone in the sales office can have an influence on profit, either contributing to greater profitability by saving expenditure or by increasing sales, or decreasing profitability by actions that lose sales or add to costs.

There are six main ways in which the sales function can influence a company's profitability. It can:

1 Increase turnover and hold costs steady.
2 Increase turnover and reduce costs.
3 Increase both turnover and costs in a controlled ratio.
4 Hold turnover steady while reducing costs.
5 Sacrifice some turnover and bring about a substantial cost reduction.
6 Alter the product mix (to favour more profitable items).

The sales function obviously plays a big part in any attempt to increase turnover, and would be instrumental in carrying out any plans to alter the product mix. It may not have so much effect on costs (beyond its own 'economy drives') if the major cost factors are manpower or materials.

The 'growth' aim of a company is closely linked with its profit aim. A decision to increase the growth rate is likely to require an increased profit, but there may not be such concern with profits if it is decided to stabilise growth. The sales function will also contribute to growth aims by such methods as the following:

(a) obtaining new customers in an existing market (e.g. prospecting activities);
(b) breaking into new markets (e.g. in support of marketing initiatives);
(c) gaining increased sales from existing accounts (e.g. by improved frequency of contact);
(d) altering the customer mix (e.g. many sales offices handle exclusively certain aspects of business with the largest and smallest customers).

The sales office, being an important part of the whole sales and distribution operation, must be fully aware of the aims of the company. The emphasis and attention it gives to its many activities, and the skill with which it carries them out, ensure that the sales office can have an immediate and considerable impact on the profitability and growth of the company.

### The sales process and the sales office

On the face of it, the process of buying something seems straightforward. But it is really a long and often complex cycle, and for repeat business it becomes a regular process capable of breaking down at any stage, and always needing attention. The successful completion of the sales process is normally the gaining of an order; but there can be a better appreciation of the factors behind selling if the sales process is regarded as only successfully completing one cycle when a repeat order is given. Then the next cycle begins.

The sales cycle is much more than face to face negotiating and selling. It is just as important for the stages to be managed properly, and for the customer to move along from one stage to the next, as it is for the salesman to carry out an effective closing of a sale.

Much of the sales office's function is concerned directly and indirectly with all stages in the sales cycle, and the office is therefore able to have an effect both on single and repeat orders.

It is often forgotten how many stages there may be in the sales process — stages where the whole process may get bogged down or end entirely. Two examples make the implications clearer.

#### Sales processes in selling repeat-purchase goods to industry

In the first example the procedure is the following:

advertising, especially in trade journals →
direct mail advertising and generating enquiries →
sales follow-up — salesman call, or supplying brochures, etc. →
ENQUIRY (e.g. by telephone) →
telephone response to telephone enquiry →
first sales interview →
proposal/quotation submitted →
telephone follow-up →
second sales interview →
CUSTOMER BUYS →
confirmation by written order →
acknowledgement of order →
provision of further information, service particulars →
delivery of goods, installation.

Naturally, not every sale has all these elements, but some sales have many more. There may be numerous sales interviews, the exchange of many letters and telephone calls, submission of revised estimates, and so on. The way in which every contact is handled, and the effect it has on the prospective customer, could make the difference between getting or losing a sale. There is every chance that the product is not unique, so it is service which can make all the difference.

The service a prospective customer gets *before* a sale influences his estimate of the service he is likely to get *after* the sale, and from the product itself. Product service and after-sales service, and the memories of pre-sales service, determine whether there will be repeat orders.

From the above example it is clear that an effectively run sales office can exert a positive influence at almost every stage. It can directly influence how an enquiry is handled, for instance, and will have an indirect effect through the support services it gives the representative in a sales interview. Alternatively, any stage badly handled may mean the customer elects to proceed no further.

*Sales processes in selling consumer goods via retailers*

This second example usually requires a dual approach — one to get retailers to stock the goods, and one to get the consumers to go in and buy them. The stages could therefore be the following:

| *Advertising promotion to consumers* | *Advertising promotion to retail trade* |
|---|---|
| response to promotions, special offers, etc. | regular call by representative |
| | merchandising/demonstration |
| enquiries | telephone sales call |
| complaints | enquiries |
| demonstrations | letter sent |
| direct sales | special representative call |
| | order given |
| | order acknowledgement |
| | delivery |

The sales office could play a part in all these stages, and could have a significant effect on sales.

*Vital contacts with the sales office*

Whatever the product is, and whoever the company's customers are, there are an increasing number of instances when the sales office, or 'inside sales people', are the only contact the customer has with the company. Rising travelling costs are only one of many factors which may make traditional representatives' calls uneconomical; and future trends in communications, such as visual displays via common telephone and TV sets, are bound to reduce the face to face sales calls still further.

There are other instances when it is far more convenient for there to be only customer/sales office contact. The following are some of them:

1    Small accounts and small orders.
2    Customers in remote locations.
3    Urgent orders.
4    'Top-up' ordering.
5    Prospecting for new business.

The sales office, therefore, not only plays an important role in the sales process, but often handles the whole sales process.

There is another form of contact when the sales office can have a deciding role in the sales process, and one which is in keeping with its support function. The 'multi-stage' selling situation, listed above, can very often extend over a long period, particularly for selling industrial goods — a few months would be very common, and a year or more is not unusual, even for items far less complex and expensive than ships, aeroplanes, specialised machine tools or computers. In such cases there is no steady progress towards buying. The buyer is periodically 'warmed up' by sales persuasion, and in between those contacts with the sales representative he will fall back in his rate of progress towards buying. Each correctly handled stage leads the buyer on to a higher point (see Figure 2.3). Sales office contact during the 'lows' can substantially flatten the curve (see Figure 2.4).

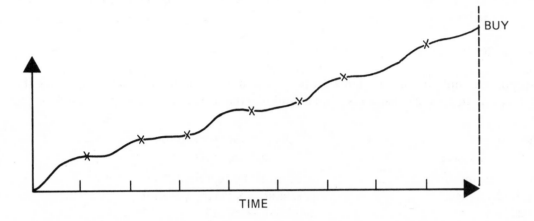

**Fig. 2.3 Progress towards a decision to buy**

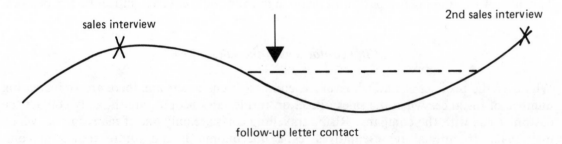

**Fig. 2.4 Sales office influence on progress towards a decision to buy**

At any stage contacts that are badly or inadequately handled may result in the customer saying 'no' and negate any chance of his proceeding further. If the sales process is long, and this happens late in the sequence of events, a considerable amount of time and money expended on progressing the customer so far will have been wasted, as well as a particular (and maybe future) sale lost. This has implications on the whole way we organise the office: for example, a lost sale can result from a new, inexperienced or badly briefed member of staff handling a customer contact at lunchtime in the absence of other personnel.

Another important factor relates to the many situations where the 'buyer' is not one man but a group or formal committee. A useful mnemonic says that the company must locate the *MAN* with the

Money<br>
Authority<br>
and    Need

which may be three (or more) people; sales office activity can help all of them towards making a positive decision to buy and make the process quicker or more certain.

These follow-ups by the sales office are not necessarily sales inputs (e.g. a telephone call or letter) designed to hasten the buying process. Routine administrative matters, even simply confirming an appointment, serve to keep the company in the buyer's mind, and will normally serve as well as positive sales action. Compromising between this view and internal administrative constraints can cause many sales office systems to founder — even those as simple as filing, for instance. An outward-looking approach, a realisation that the sales office can have influence, will see many opportunities for advancing the sales decision.

A company which appreciates the role of a sales office will ensure that there is an overlap with all other administrative functions which affect customers — quotations should never be done separately from the sales office, and there should be some contact over the delivery process. After the sale, invoices and statements (and such troublesome things as letters to late payers) should not be done in total isolation from the sales office.

### Sales management, the sales force, and the sales office

We have seen that marketing is organising the company to meet the consumers' needs, and have looked at the sales office's role in marketing. The sales process and the way the sales office can influence it have been examined.

What about the main 'tactical weapon' a company can use to achieve the marketing strategy — the sales force? Sales management has the responsibility for the sales force and for achieving the sales target set in accordance with marketing policy. Where does the sales office fit in? It frequently comes under the control of sales management, and is often in very close (though not always amicable) contact with the outside sales force; understanding the proper role of the members of the sales force is important before we can appreciate their relationship with a sales office. Unfortunately this is often misunderstood, and the benefits that a company can derive from a fully constructive relationship are left unexploited.

The basic role of sales management is to achieve sales revenue results through other people. In carrying out its role it has six key responsibilities:

1  Planning strategy and tactics.
2  Organising activities.
3  Controlling activities.
4  Selection of sales people to carry out tasks.
5  Development of sales people, particularly on the job.
6  Motivation of sales people.

Since it achieves results through people, the development and motivation of people are the most important of the sales management's responsibilities. Unfortunately, however, we all know many cases where sales management only concentrates on the two activities of selling and administration (and sometimes on only one of these), and the results of this concentration will nearly always affect the sales office.

The sales force is the main tactical weapon in the marketing armoury, and its efficiency is absolutely critical to the success of the whole enterprise. Very often the only difference between competitors is the quality of their sales force; the company with the best planned, selected, trained, motivated and controlled sales force will dominate the market. There is no other activity in a company where inefficiency and lack of effort and quality will have such immediate effect, and none which can so easily be managed and manipulated to alter the fortunes of the company. No wonder the sales force often seeks and sometimes gets the glamour and the quick acclaim!

But the sales force cannot do everything. It cannot operate on its own, and it is often not the most cost-effective system available.

The sales office itself can have a number of advantages over the sales force, apart from being the sales force's essential support. For example, it is often superior in the following ways:

1  *Speed/coverage* — customer contact can be much faster since it does not have to be face to face; therefore more customers can be contacted in a short time.

2  *Control* — a sales force is scattered and difficult to make quick contact with, so is difficult to control. The resources of a sales office are centralised and can be directed to react immediately according to changing events.

3  *Cost* — it costs a lot to keep a salesman 'on the road', often more than £15,000 a year, and as it is not unusual for a salesman to spend the minority of his time, perhaps only 15-20 per cent, in face to face contact with clients, the cost per call is therefore very high. (The figure of £15,000 is an average; for many it may be higher. It includes not only salary but also commission, car, operating costs and an allowance for recruitment training, administrative support and management time.)

4  *Order pattern* — many businesses have a 'seasonal pattern' which can be awkward to cope with; the timing of orders affects many things from cash flow to production planning and wages, but a well-planned sales office can smooth the effects by its speed, coverage, and cost per call advantage.

However, the sales office should not be regarded as an alternative to the sales force, but as an operation which can work with the sales force to support and consolidate the sales process at many stages. A constructive relationship with sales management and the field sales force can be very valuable, though it may well need to be worked for; any initiative taken by the sales office to this end can be most productive, and help create a climate where the process becomes two-way.

*Summary*

'Marketing', as opposed to simply 'selling' is vital for the survival of a business.

'Service' determines the success of a company in highly competitive industries where products and prices have become similar.

The role of the sales staff as a whole, both internal and external, working together, is a vital tactical one as part of the marketing strategy. To be effective in this role, the sales office must have:

1  A full awareness of company aims.
2  A clear understanding of the functions the department must fulfil.
3  Complete confidence in the company's products and services.
4  Full product knowledge, which it understands and can put across in customer terms.

# Part Two

# Managing and Controlling Sales Office Activity

# 3: Setting Up the Organisation

Part II of this book is concerned as much with the right attitude to the administrative side of the activity as with how to carry out particular tasks. If the administration is to be kept as a means to an end, rather than becoming an end in itself, this is important. It will help ensure that the office has sufficient time to action and progress matters relating directly to achieving additional sales or maintaining ongoing business.

Organising sales office activity requires at the outset that there is an understanding of all the activities that can go on. The nature and scale of the activities in a sales office derive from a matrix which can be represented by that in Figure 3.1.

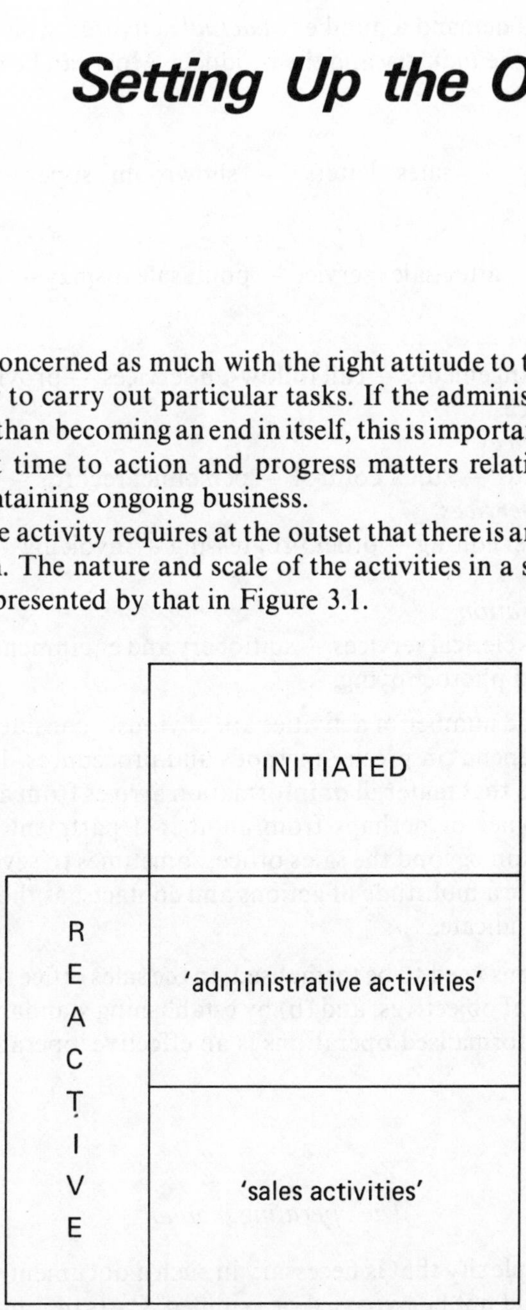

Fig. 3.1 The nature of sales office activity

Initiated activities define those begun with the sales office, while reactive activities are those that happen purely as the result of outside stimulus. The following are examples:

*Reactive selling* — handling an incoming enquiry, by, for instance, sending a brochure or a price list, or simply giving details over the telephone.

*Reactive/administrative* — updating records after receiving stock reports, and recording sales figures.

*Initiated/selling* — a follow-up sales letter, a reminder about an appointment, sending new product information, or telephone canvassing for new customers.

*Initiated/administrative* — informing a representative about an enquiry, or passing on information about competitive products or prices.

These types of action will demand a number of *actual* activities, which vary from company to company, depending on the industry and the products. Most can be covered by the following six headings and examples:

1 *Direct selling*
   Telephone selling — sales letters — showroom supervision — exhibitions — demonstrations.

2 *Customer services*
   Enquiry services — after-sales service — point sale display — arrangements — mailing list maintenance.

3 *Field force services*
   Appointment arrangements — call follow-up services — provision of sales material — information services.

4 *Management services*
   Statistics — records — stock control — personnel records — scheduling.

5 *Order fulfilment services*
   Estimating — order editing — order progressing — invoicing — transport and shipping — installation.

6 *General administration*
   Typing services — clerical services — stationery and equipment — mail sorting — filing — duplicating and photocopying.

The work required and the number of activities are obviously considerable, and it is clear that efficient running must depend on precise methods and procedures. In general, action means 'progressing', in the sense that material or information arrives from a source outside the sales office — from the customer or perhaps from another department — action is taken, and something is then passed on beyond the sales office, sometimes to several destinations. Even a simple task can necessitate a multitude of actions and contacts, as the examples in Figure 3.2, based on this sequence, indicate.

Such complex operations need to be formalised. In the sales office this is usually done in two ways: (a) by setting formal objectives; and (b) by establishing standard operating procedures. The best foundation for formalised operations is an effective 'operating manual'.

*The operating manual*

While the detail and complexity that is necessary in such a document will vary, it does fulfil an important role, and should not be bypassed or skimped. Parts of it may need to be explicit — bordering on the pedantic — to get the message across. Compiling, extending or reviewing

20

**Example 1  Customer enquiries**

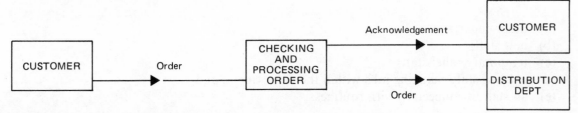

**Example 2  Processing orders**

**Example 3  Analysing representatives' reports**

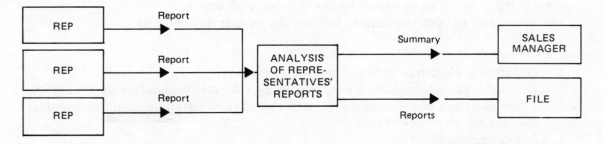

**Example 4  Up-dating sales promotional material**

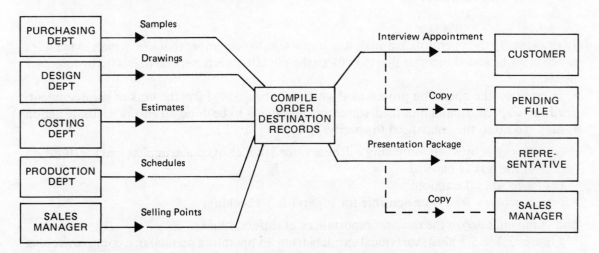

Fig. 3.2  The sequence of sales office activity

such a document can be delegated throughout a section, with each individual sharing in the writing and the manager 'editing'. In this way it need not be a very time-consuming exercise.

A manual should be a manager's essential aid in organising his own activity, and that of the whole department. It can be as important for complex as for routine tasks, but should begin by listing objectives. Knowing what the department has been set up to do gives everyone a greater sense of commitment, creates team working, and can contribute significantly to giving mundane tasks some degree of purpose. Knowing why a job is done is the first step to doing it better.

This is vital in a section impacting on sales results. For example, neither a specialist producing an estimate, nor the secretary originating the letter to go with it, will do so in a way likely to maximise the chance of its leading to a sale if they view it as simply a technical, administrative or secretarial task. The manual can put the task in context — as a sales activity — and ensure more effective results.

A manual can be used as a reference by:

(a)  other departments;
(b)  new staff;
(c)  temporary relief staff;
(d)  existing staff changing jobs within the department; and
(e)  all staff in connection with routines.

All these need to know the objectives of the department, and it is important that all activities covered in the manual can be seen to be linked to these objectives.

The contents of an operating manual can usefully include the following:

1   Department objectives, activities and responsibilities.
2   Detailed organisation charts for the marketing/sales division, and for the sales office.
3   Organising chart of the company. (Charts should show operating relationships rather than the hierarchy downwards.)
4   Job descriptions.
5   Operating procedures.
6   Standing instructions.

In drawing up the operating manual, it is important to remember that everything in the sales office must be stated in terms that (a) link to the overall objectives, and (b) relate to customer needs.

In addition the operating procedures, which will probably form the bulk of the document, need to be specific enough in their statement of *what* is to be done, to ensure accurate action results. To do so they may need to specify:

(a)  *timing* — by when something will be actioned (which of course implies that the duration of the task is known);
(b)  *who* will take action;
(c)  *control* — who is responsible for supervising/checking;

and comment also on the relative importances of different tasks.

Figures 3.3 to 3.8 illustrate typical extracts from an operating manual in a company selling office record systems.

VISCARD RECORD SYSTEMS LIMITED

SALES OFFICE OBJECTIVES

1. *Direct Sales*
   To maintain a six-monthly contact by telephone or letter with all purchasers of Viscard Record Systems in order to:

   1. Obtain repeat stationery orders.
   2. Extend the applications of customer's current systems.
   3. Introduce new systems and make arrangements for demonstrations by representatives.

2. *Customer Services*
   To provide customers with:

   1. A fully equipped showroom at head office, ensuring that a demonstrator is available at all times.
   2. A same-day answer on all written enquiries.
   3. Technical and service advice by telephone from 9.00 a.m. to 5.30 p.m. Monday—Friday.
   4. The names of agencies in their area who will undertake updating and data transfer services.

3. *Field Force Services*
   1. To ensure that all representatives receive full product information, modification details, samples and promotion literature immediately it becomes available.
   2. To circularise all representatives with details of new applications of existing Viscard products discovered by other representatives.
   3. To provide same-day service on all written and telephoned enquiries or queries from the field force.

4. *Sales Management Services*
   To provide on the last day of each month an analysis of:

   1. Representatives' calls, orders, costs.
   2. Volume of orders placed for each line.
   3. Current orders outstanding.
   4. Enquiries received and outcome.
   5. Complaints received and outcome.

5. *Order Fulfilment*
   1. To provide estimates within 48 hours.
   2. To examine all orders and pass to Production Department by 4.30 p.m. on the day of receipt.
   3. To progress all orders and advise the customer and representative of despatch date.

6. *General Administration*
   1. To provide and maintain the administrative, clerical and secretarial services necessary for the efficient operation of the sales division within prescribed cost budgets.
   2. To be responsible for the purchase and maintenance of all equipment used by the sales division, internally or in the field.

**Fig. 3.3  Operating manual: departmental objectives, activities and responsibilities**

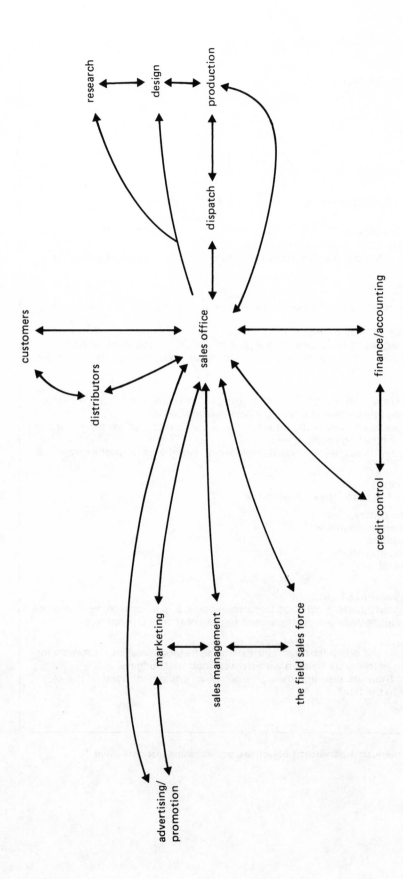

research    design    production

dispatch

customers

sales office

distributors

finance/accounting

credit control

marketing

sales management

the field sales force

advertising/
promotion

Note (i) This shows sales office contact only.

(ii) In a large organisation both company and departmental organisation charts may be useful as well.

**Fig. 3.4 Operating manual: contact chart**

*Format*

```
Job Title: _____

Department/Section: _____

Responsible to: _____

Responsible for:        key job objectives

              1. _____

              2. _____

              3. _____


Duties:
```

**Fig. 3.5 Operating manual: job descriptions**

Job descriptions can be usefully included for all members of a section (even if it needs a separate version from personnel — without, for example, salary information so that everyone can refer to them). If you do not have a job description or have anyone reporting to you without one, not only does this make aspects of management very difficult, it links with various aspects of recent employment legislation which can cause problems. For example, it may be very difficult to terminate someone's employment when they do not have one. This may be an important area on which the reader should separately update.

*Operating Procedures*

*Function*    To provide customer information.

*Objective*    To answer every customer's enquiry, providing the latest product information, up-to-date prices and details of 3 local stockists, on the day the enquiry is received.

In defining this objective 5 points of performance measurement are established:

What must    To answer *every* customer enquiry.
be done       To provide the *latest* product information.
               To provide *up-to-date* prices.
               To name *3* local stockists.

by when    to provide the *same-day* service.

by whom    Actioned by sales co-ordinator responsible for geographic area.

*Priority* A

Control    copy letter to representative
              enquiries for £x+ to be seen by office manager

**Fig. 3.6  Operating manual: operating procedures**

While all operating procedures need to be entirely explicit and some need to be written along the lines above, many can be demonstrated by example. The manual can, for instance, contain enquiry forms, complaint forms, invoices, dispatch notes, estimates etc., showing both how they are completed and used. This simplifies the description and means different items can be prepared by different people (see Figure 3.6). Alternatively, activities can be described graphically in network analysis style, which can add clarity (see Figure 3.8).

Many of the steps in these operating procedures demand the completion of complex forms; computer-based operations in particular require accurate and consistent documentation. The manual should always contain completed examples of all the forms used in these circumstances, so that guidance given is clear and comprehensive.

A final area of contents, that of standing instructions, may seem unimportant but it is worth including here company policies and departmental rules, on such matters as time keeping, notification of sickness, time off, telephone calls, dress, approval of different levels of expenditure, duty rotas, times of postage collection etc. Some of these, if unclear, can lose sales, e.g. a letter missing the post. Others can result in internal friction or strife unless understood. All must be updated or their relevance can lapse: for example, a change in office layout may expose new people to visiting customers, with implications on dress.

Many sales offices run on the accumulated memory of their members, but an operating manual means that almost any new arrival can quickly be effective, and with the least disruption to the rest of the staff, who otherwise would constantly be interrupted to explain procedures. Obviously the manual must be kept up to date, since procedures have the habit of evolving, and such gradual modifications will only complicate matters if they are not incorporated into the manual, and are not followed by new staff. A loose-leaf format makes this more straightforward.

## TELEPHONE MESSAGE

FOR: Name: **B. Wright**     Date: **10/1/80**

Department: **Sales Office**     Time: **4·20 p.m.**

From:

Name: **P. Forsyth**     Title: **Client Services Director**

Company: **Marketing Improvements Ltd**

Address: **Ulster House**
**17 Ulster Terrace, Regents Park Outer Circle,**
**London NW1**

Telephone: **01 487 5811**     Telex: **299723**

About: **Information on new product.**
**Model X37**

Action taken: **Product literature sent**

Action promised: **You to telephone on 13/1/80**

Message taken by: **A.N.O.**     ext **37**

Fig. 3.7  Operating manual: operating procedures/demonstration by specimen form

# NETWORK ANALYSIS AND FLOW CHART FOR ANSWERING CUSTOMER ENQUIRIES AND UPDATING INFORMATION FILES

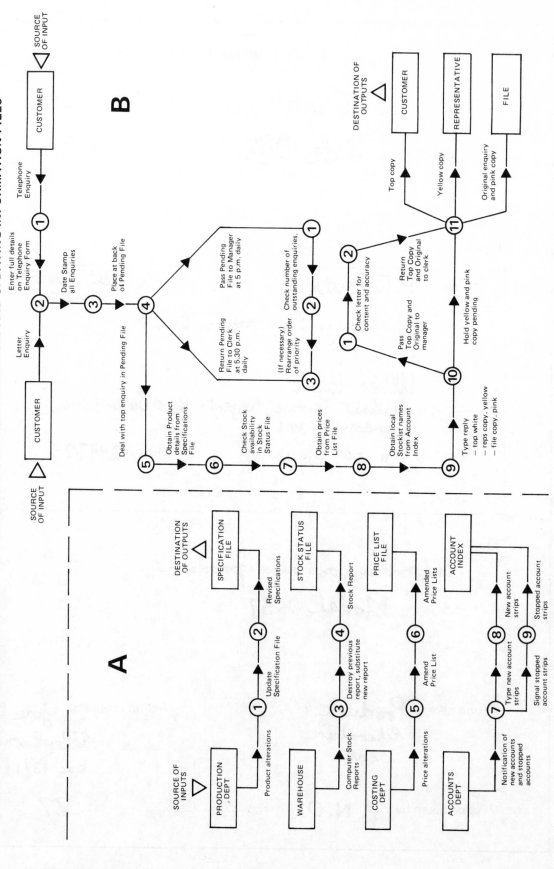

Fig. 3.8 Operating manual: operating procedures/graphic demonstration in network analysis style

At the same time it is important not to let the manual become sacrosanct. It is an essential aid to training, to memory and to settling uncertainties, but a slavish following of its 'rules' would prevent the evolution of improved procedures. It must be a 'working' manual, one that is used regularly, not an impersonal compendium of rules and regulations. Including in it some separate and regularly used sets of information, e.g. about products or prices, will help ensure it is used and does not gather dust on the shelf. An understanding that systems and procedures can, indeed must, be changed, and that everyone can contribute to the establishment of better procedures, which will be incorporated into the manual, will encourage a sense of participation, which is important to motivation.

# 4:

# Managing Time

Unless the company is rapidly declining, a sales office is one of the busiest departments, and seldom does a day end without some work being left undone. Ways must be found of making best use of time available if we are to achieve what we want and do so effectively. One way to get through each day's quota is to organise a rigid system of priorities (and stick to it). Another is to arrange careful and realistic scheduling.

## *Priorities*

Since sales office work consists of reactive and initiated activity, as well as of routine recording and production of information, some system of priorities is essential, especially in relation to the large number of documents and papers that are passed between people and departments. At all times direct response to customers would normally require immediate attention, at least deserving an 'important' label.

It would be useful, for example, to institute a system of four categories, A, B, C and D, perhaps standing for 'essential', 'important', 'useful', and 'when time available'. Some companies use a particularly descriptive last category — WPB (standing for wastepaper basket).

The operating manual should include this classification, with the everyday items that belong in the various categories (see Figure 3.6). On 'one off' items the sales office manager would use his judgement. An article about one of the company's products being used in a remote part of the world might be classed as 'useful', for photocopying and distributing to representatives, unless it was thought it could help clinch a current negotiation, in which case it would be given an 'essential' label. Requests for quotations would obviously be 'essential', requiring immediate attention. Notification of a stock adjustment might be 'important', and so on.

The thing to remember about a priority system is that its rules should be adhered to. If something is 'essential', then it must be done by the time specified. Preparation of the monthly sales summary is an essential sales office task, which has to be done even if everyone works all weekend doing it.

At the other end of the scale, there should be some effort to deal with the 'when time available' file on a regular basis — time must be made to be available. If there never is a moment to deal with 'desirable but not essential' matters, then either the department is being inefficiently run or is understaffed (which is seldom the cost saving that management hopes it will be, and in the long run has a detrimental effect on the company).

Another useful weapon to use in the battle to find enough time is to get everyone (yourself included) to mark paperwork 'urgent', 'read', 'reply', 'record', 'discuss', or with similar classifications. This is far better than the usual in/out/pending, and will allow a better use of time available. It avoids the repeated mental classification that is necessary when a whole batch of paperwork has to be flipped through every time a few minutes are available.

It is also a very useful system to have when one of the staff is away from the office, as it makes it much easier for someone else to carry on with the outstanding work. If equipment is matched to this approach and every desk has the same it is even easier to locate work in progress.

## *Scheduling*

In every sales office there are at any time many, often conflicting or overlapping, 'deadlines' to be met.

A schedule lays down the precise timing and sequence of events in the execution of a plan. For many jobs, schedules are essential. Promotion material required by the sales force to back up an advertising campaign, for instance, could require a lot of preparation. Without a schedule there would be a great deal of ineffectual rushing about, briefing printers, copywriters and photographers, and inevitably it would all be late.

By far the best way to prepare most schedules is to work backwards from the target date. If the results of a survey of customers are required by a certain date, list everything that has to be done, and how long each stage will take (see Figure 4.1).

|  | Action | Days |
|---|---|---|
| Target: | Present analysis | 1 |
|  | Analyse replies | 3 |
|  | Customers fill in questionnaire and return | 12 |
|  | Questionnaires sent by post | 3 |
|  | Address envelope and insert questionnaires | 1 |
|  | Print questionnaires and covering letters | 4 |
| Begin: | Draw up questionnaire and covering letter | 4 |
|  |  | 28 |
|  | Days lost by weekends/public holidays | 9 |
|  | Total days required | 37 (+ contingency) |

**Fig. 4.1  Scheduling backwards to meet deadlines**

If there are only 31 days left before the analysis is required, it will be immediately obvious that it is an unrealistic request; either it should be modified, or the schedule should be examined to see if 6 days can be saved. If not, the time to admit that it is impossible is *now*. There is nothing to be gained by trying to keep to an unrealistic schedule.

Attempts to streamline the schedule should not be too desperate. Allowance should always be made for 'Murphy's Laws', which remind us that things are always (a) more complicated than you think, (b) take more time than you think they will, and (c) cost more than you think they will. It is also as well to have some respect for 'Sod's Law', which warns that if something can go wrong, it will.

With any complex project we should add some additional 'contingency' time. An honest schedule will avoid the need for 'firefighting', rushed decisions and last minute changes, with all their attendant dangers.

### Using time properly

The third element in time management is how well we use the time that is available. Everyone's day has 24 hours, and the difference between the successful and the less successful is often simply how those hours are managed.

The sales office is a place where the unexpected is always happening. There is no control over who is suddenly going to telephone with a complaint, a query, or an order. Work is constantly being interrupted by some matter that requires a higher priority, and it is difficult to get a routine to run smoothly without establishing a work pattern that only allows anyone to do one or two tasks, which in turn leads to boredom and a high turnover of staff.

Because unscheduled activities are so common, it is very easy to abandon all intentions to organise a work plan. But if only a small percentage of our time is not reactive and therefore able to be planned (see Figure 4.2), the logic must be that there is even more reason to do the planning, not that it is impossible.

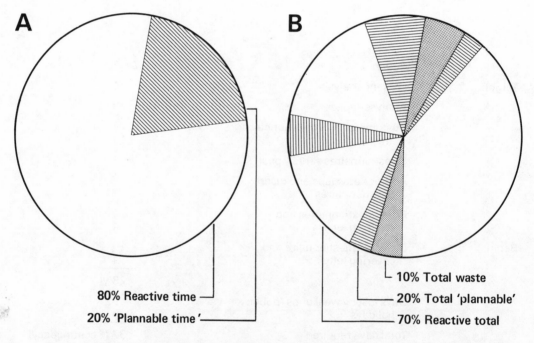

Note: More likely as in B the 'plannable' ▤ time will occur at random throughout our day.
Add an amount for an element of wasted time. ▦

**Fig. 4.2 Planning our time**

Remember G.K. Chesterton's remark, writing about Christianity, that 'it is not that it has been tried and found wanting, it is that it has been found difficult and therefore not tried'. So it is with time planning. It is important, therefore, to develop a habit and a formula to ensure we beat this problem. Without this we may achieve a very inefficient use of the time available.

There are three commonsense steps that will lead to a better use of time, however varied or unexpected the activities:

1. *Plan priorities regularly*, and put them in writing. If there are a large number of interruptions every day, plan a way of dealing with them. For instance, it may be better only to process telephone orders after 3.00 p.m., for nothing might be gained by doing so earlier. By taking down the minimum required information at the time, there will be minimum disruption to the job in hand. Regular planning keeps an important element of flexibility, and prevents one having to try to account for every eventuality. It means only a few minutes a day.

2. *Do what the plan says*. Having taken the trouble to plan, follow the plan. Spur of the moment decisions to abandon the plan will mean that urgent matters will always take precedence over important ones. This is a constant clash in business, but the favouring of urgent over important is wasteful. Once the habit is started, more and more matters are judged to be urgent, and the important things never get done. Above all, changing the plan will sooner or later mean procrastinating, e.g. leaving till last things we like doing least, and in a sales office, with so much to do, that it as good as abandoning them.

3. *Establish when action is to be taken*. This is the good side of procrastination. Apply it to actions and decisions, and a lot of time spent on worrying can be avoided. If something does not need a decision or action for another 3 days, perhaps until certain information is available as the basis for a decision, there is no point in mulling it over until then. Events might overtake a decision made prematurely, and that will have been a complete waste of time and effort. Dealing with things only when it is necessary avoids time wasted shuffling priorities and on simply 'sitting worrying'.

All the above sounds simple. It is simpler to write or read, however, than to do. Yet it really is a vital factor both in success for a particular individual in his job and in organising a team within a sales office section.

# 5: Managing Systems

Business methods and circumstances change more quickly than ever today, and, whether because of technology or market forces, this is likely to continue. It has been said, with some truth, that 'if your system works well, it is obsolete'; and certainly an attitude that questions every format and procedure and is able — with an open mind — to accept change necessitated by outside influences is a vital characteristic of the sales office manager.

The systems that concern a sales office are mainly to do with information, and in this section we look primarily at storing information. The sales office has to be a considerable storehouse of information, and a great deal more passes through its hands as well. Information will be in one or more of the following categories:

1 Product information.
2 Company information.
3 Prices/terms.
4 Customer information.
5 Statistical information.
6 Competitor information.

Since it is impossible to know all the information necessary to carry out a job, the next best thing is to know how to get hold of it. This assumes knowing what information is available, where to find it, and, not least, being able to find it. A haphazard system means that no one will know what information it might or might not contain; an illogical system will result in no one knowing where to look; and a messy, overloaded system will prevent anyone finding what they are looking for.

*Electronic systems*

In an effort to overcome these common obstacles, technology has produced many developments. The availability of computers or computer time-sharing was the first step, but this has mainly meant that it is easier to keep more information, and to retrieve it more quickly than before and in numerous permutations.

Variations of this produced visual display terminals, and more or less simultaneously other developments brought the microfilm and microfiche. With a little sophisticated equipment, it is now possible to view enormous amounts of information only a few minutes, even seconds, after deciding it is needed.

The most recent developments in microprocessors and silicon chip technology do have the potential for making significant impacts on every activity, sales offices included, and it would be shortsighted to pretend that such developments are only feasible 'in theory' — the companies that ignore them will steadily lose their position in the market place. Simple and inexpensive devices carried by representatives or used by customers already allow direct links between telephone and television and the company's computer. No matter where he is (as long as a phone and TV set are available) the representative will be able to have an up-to-the-minute visual display of available stocks, delivery time, prices and discounts; he will then be able to record an order, place an immediate delivery instruction, have the order processed, an invoice dispatched, stock level amended, and so on. In some industries this much is happening now.

Currently 'silicon chip technology' is making everything small — putting it on the desk top, in fact — and less expensive. The future in this area is both full of opportunity and rather frightening (see Figure 5.1).

MANUFACTURER: My customers sit at home comparing my products with those of my competitors on their visual display units. To help them make up their minds they call up the latest consumer advice reports. They check which distributors offer the best prices, promotions and which have stock available. Then they place their order through their visual display unit and get acknowledgement. At the same time either their bank account is debited or a credit check undertaken, before order acceptance is signified and delivery time given.

CUSTOMER: And the consumer has not left his armchair.

**Fig. 5.1 A technological scenario**

But the very qualities of computer systems have often turned out to be liabilities. The impressive ease with which vast amounts of paper can be 'reduced' to a collection of small cards, or to a few feet on a magnetic tape (and be recalled at will), generally means that far too much information is stored, with no saving in costs (electronic or optical storage systems are expensive) or, eventually, in time either. Not only is too much stored, but too much is retrieved also, and instead of simplifying life, it makes it more complicated, if a little more glamorous to begin with. Computer and microphotographic systems, therefore, are not miracle workers, and the same principles must be applied to them as are applied to purely manual systems.

No matter what 'automatic' system is used, the human element is always needed — machines must be 'fed' and someone must still think for them from time to time. Very often the sales office has little choice in what automated system has to be used — it is generally chosen for a number of primary tasks — and that makes it doubly important to avoid the two great evils in storing information: duplication and continuing to maintain 'one-off' information.

*Duplication*

Often a number of record systems are in use and information is duplicated: for example, information on customer records. A simple matrix will soon show if duplication is occurring and allow rationalisation (see Figure 5.2).

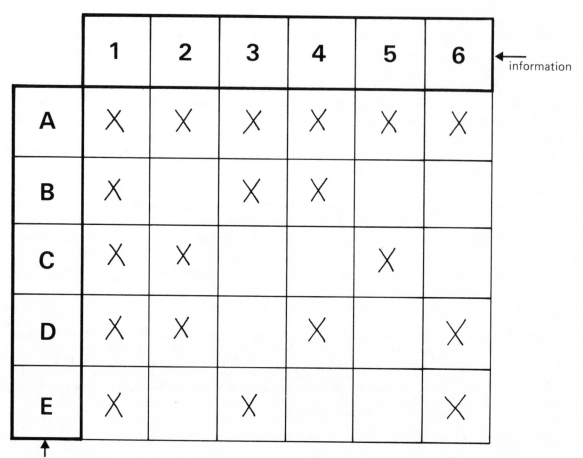

|   | 1 | 2 | 3 | 4 | 5 | 6 |
|---|---|---|---|---|---|---|
| A | X | X | X | X | X | X |
| B | X |   | X | X |   |   |
| C | X | X |   |   | X |   |
| D | X | X |   | X |   | X |
| E | X |   | X |   |   | X |

← information

↑ record system

Note:   Matching where information is recorded with how it is usually accessed will produce savings. For example, if information 4 is usually looked for in system A, does it need to be in B and D?

**Fig. 5.2 Checking for duplicated information**

*Continuing to maintain 'one-off' information*

Without checking, this can lead to the kind of situation where information is being produced for nothing. For example, a managing director asks for a special analysis of certain major customers' sales figures, and he is duly sent them, not once but every month for the next two years. Only when the files with his secretary are checked is it noticed that they have never, after the first time, gone further than her desk. They were only wanted the first time. Easily done — but easy to check.

It is also essential (especially when the vast capacities of electronic systems are being considered) to remember that information is only important for what it can do, not for what it is.

One final pitfall of computer-based information is its perceived accuracy. We look at a figure like 110,543.12764 (i.e. to five places of decimals) and conclude it must be accurate. However, if it is a forecast with an actual identified margin of error of +/− 10 per cent, then we must view it differently (and maybe write it as 110,500 in the first place).

*Filing*

For the majority of sales offices, information means files, but the habits that lead to an efficient filing system will also get the most out of a computer system.

The most useful dictum that can be applied to filing is, 'Is this needed again?' If the answer is 'no', then why file it? Researches have indicated that only 10 per cent of filed matter is ever used again, which means that 90 per cent is useless. The problem, of course, is knowing which 10 per cent will be used, but better filing should easily reduce the 'useless' files to 50 or 60 per cent.

Modern, automated, computerised, electronic, microphotographic filing systems do not alter the ratio of used again to never used again. The major difference is that they take up less space, and cost more.

There are two ways to reduce the amount of useless filing: (a) do not file, and (b) 'clean' the files regularly. Filing on the offchance that it may be needed one day, often for the wrong reasons, e.g. to protect ourselves in case something goes wrong, can very often turn out more expensive than re-originating the information should it eventually be required. 'When in doubt, don't file' could be the right approach.

The important things about filing are what to file, and how to file, bearing in mind that a bad system is cluttered up with too much irrelevant material, and no one can ever find what they want.

*What to file*

The decision on what to file is a responsible one. It should be done with consistency as well, so it must be established which people should be responsible for filing decisions — they should be fairly senior staff. This may well mean the manager, who must not see the filing tray as an easy means of clearing his desk, rather than the secretary, who may be a person whose attitude is, 'Do you want this again, or shall I file it?'

The following are useful hints to remember when trying to reduce the amount that is to be filed:

*Hold for a period, then 'clean' vigorously*. At the time information is first dealt with, it seems important. After a week, or a month, it gets into better perspective. In the meantime, use a category to keep it in (see next section, 'How to file'), or simply have an alphabetical file. When filing day comes around, the 'filer' should be certain that the document is worth keeping before it is given the appropriate notation. What is uncertain or unlikely must not be filed.

If day files are kept, they should not be allowed to worm their way into permanent files, but should be destroyed at regular dates — the last day of each month, for instance, could be the day to destroy the day file for that month a year before.

*File only what is essential*. The reports of a meeting may be filed, but not the memos announcing it, where it will be held, the notes made to prepare for it.

*Simplify internal memos*. The use of 'ping pong' memos, with space for handwritten replies, not only simplifies and speeds up internal correspondence, but makes a lot of filing unnecessary. The question and answer are together, and if that is the end of the matter, then destroy the memo and your original duplicate.

*How to file*

A file that cannot be found is useless, and alphabetical filing under logical categories will make access for everyone a lot easier. By keeping them simple, the same categories can be used for the holding period as for the long-term files, categories could include current projects, past transactions, current information, and continuous records.

A key file in a sales office is the 'prompt', or bring forward file. Keeping two of these — one for the regular jobs, such as updating records, and one for one-off material — will avoid making anyone go through a big pending tray every day, or having to rely on memory. If some item in the one-off prompt file cannot be resolved when it comes up, then it can be put back again to come up at a later date. This file can be designed to raise the matter again on a specific date or in one week, two weeks, one month, three months, or at any more suitable intervals. It can also act as a 'parking' file, and when documents have been dealt with, they should be given a critical eye before filing more permanently.

# 6:                                                    *Controlling*

One of the most important functions of sales management is controlling the activities of the sales force, and this is another task where the sales office plays a vital supporting role. It is often the sales office which supplies the information essential to control. It is not concerned with the controlling task itself, but it can often initiate controlling decisions.

There are a large number of items which need control, and this control means examining facts and figures relating to such matters as turnover, unit sales, expense budgets, and representatives' calls. The facts and figures are assembled by the sales office. Some will have come originally from the accounts division, some will be taken from computer print-outs, and some will come from the representatives themselves, in the form of daily, weekly or monthly reports.

It is not simply a matter of assembling information and passing it on, however. As with so much numerical and statistical information, the figures used for controlling are on their own relatively useless. What really counts is their comparison with other figures, so it is the 'variance' that is essential to control.

The important figures used for comparison are called 'standards' — often they are targets — while previous figures for a similar, earlier period are also commonly used. Control, therefore, is the simple task of assessing actual performance against pre-set standards, and analysing the variance. This can be expressed in terms of the formula

$$A - S = V (+ \text{ or } -)$$

where A = actual performance, S = standards and V = variance.

## Standards

The essential elements in controlling, therefore, are the standards. These are set by management in accordance with the budgets and plans drawn up by the company. There are three types of standards — absolute, moving and diagnostic.

*Absolute standards*

Absolute standards are primarily standards of control, and the most common one would be the annual sales target. Achievement of this standard is the conventional definition of success, but such an absolute standard is only measured when it is too late to take any action on it. It indicates what has happened, good or bad, after it happens, and gives an indication why it happened. An unsophisticated fire alarm in a computer room is unlikely to prevent damage or indicate the cause of the fire — actual flames would be the alarm's absolute standard.

*Moving standards*

Moving standards represent a more sophisticated approach, by measuring monthly, weekly or even daily sales performance against target. Variances are therefore noticed a lot sooner, and attention would be drawn to an abnormal situation. However, there would have to be further investigation to find out why the variance occurred. An abnormal temperature warning would signal the possibility of serious fire developing in the computer room, and severe damage could be prevented — but it would not pinpoint the cause of the rising temperature.

*Diagnostic standards*

Diagnostic standards, such as call rates, call frequencies, types of call indicating customer mix, prospecting rate, and many types of ratios (e.g. calls/orders), are designed to indicate why performance and target are at variance. The manager may therefore decide for himself exactly what affects performance and so specify the appropriate diagnostic standards. Again, as with any standards, it is the variance which is important.

Once the standards have been set by the management, they are recorded by the sales office, and then the relevant performance figures are collected and collated. In many instances the reporting of performance is only done when it reaches a level outside a certain tolerance around the expected standard. Further on in this chapter we look at this principle which is called 'management by exception'. Once the variances have been pinpointed by the sales office, it is management's job to select and implement whatever corrective measures are required.

### Collecting the information

Technological developments, which have made it easier and easier to collect and process vast amounts of data, have often made management and control more difficult, not less. There is scarcely a manager who does not complain about the amount of paperwork and figures that have to be handled every day, and it is getting worse. The trouble is that information is too often assembled simply because it exists. It is never worse than when a company has new computer facilities; to justify the expenditure the system is made to produce information which few people have the time to analyse or assess, or the ability to use constructively.

Information collection must start with the setting of only the standards that really are necessary. The standards must be clearly defined. The information then collected should only be information that is relevant to those standards.

Although it is not the sales office's job to determine what information sales management should see, if it ever makes a suggestion it should be for supplying less information. A sales office manager should, in fact, resist the temptation to make his division seem more important by the production of more and more unnecessary facts and figures. Being able to come up with detailed information fairly rapidly from time to time is one thing: producing an endless stream of it is another.

*Monitoring the information.*

The following Examples 1-12 demonstrate how, with simple mathematics, the same figures can reveal different trends and variances, depending on the purpose they are used for, and the method of analysis used. Applications are equally valid for products, customers, unit sales, cash sales, salesmen's calls, budgets, forecasts analysed over specific periods etc. (*Note.* Brackets are set round negative or minus figures; this is accounting practice and aids identification. The headings 2+/–1 etc. mean year 2 above or below year 1 etc.)

*Example 1*

*To isolate variances.* Each quarterly figure is set down as it occurs and is then compared to the like period in the previous year.

|  | Actual Year | | | Variance Year | |
|---|---|---|---|---|---|
|  | 1 | 2 | 3 | 2+/–1 | 3+/–2 |
| 1st quarter | 2 | 3 | 7 | 1 | 4 |
| 2nd quarter | 5 | 9 | 4 | 4 | (5) |
| 3rd quarter | 4 | 4 | 7 | — | 3 |
| 4th quarter | 7 | 9 | 8 | 2 | (1) |
| Total | 18 | 25 | 26 | 7 | 1 |

*Example 2*

*To isolate cumulative variance.* Each quarterly figure is added to the previous cumulative figure and then compared to the like period in the previous year.

|  | Actual Year | | | Variance Year | |
|---|---|---|---|---|---|
|  | 1 | 2 | 3 | 2+/–1 | 3+/–2 |
| 1st quarter | 2 | 3 | 7 | 1 | 4 |
| 2nd quarter | 7 | 12 | 11 | 5 | (1) |
| 3rd quarter | 11 | 16 | 18 | 5 | 2 |
| 4th quarter | 18 | 25 | 26 | 7 | 1 |

*Example 3*

*To establish an average.* The total to date is divided by the number of months.

|  | Actual | | | | |
|---|---|---|---|---|---|
|  | Jan. | Feb. | Mar. | Total | Monthly average |
| Mr A | 2 | 3 | 7 | 12 | 4 |
| Mr B | 5 | 9 | 4 | 18 | 6 |
| Mr C | 4 | 4 | 7 | 15 | 5 |
| Mr D | 7 | 9 | 8 | 24 | 8 |
| Total | 18 | 25 | 26 | 69 | 23 |

*Example 4*

*To establish a trend by averages.* The cumulative to date is divided by the number of months, at the end of each month.

|  | *Actual* | | | *Trend* | | |
|---|---|---|---|---|---|---|
|  | Jan. | Feb. | Mar. | Jan. | Feb. | Mar. |
| Mr A | 2 | 3 | 7 | 2 | 2½ | 4 |
| Mr B | 5 | 9 | 4 | 5 | 7 | 6 |
| Mr C | 4 | 4 | 7 | 4 | 4 | 5 |
| Mr D | 7 | 9 | 8 | 7 | 8 | 8 |

*Example 5*

*To compare performance against forecast* and the like period in the previous year.

|  | Year 2 | Year 3 Budget | Year 3 Actual | Actual +/− Budget | Actual +/− Year 2 |
|---|---|---|---|---|---|
| Week 1 | 2 | 3 | 7 | 4 | 5 |
| Week 2 | 5 | 9 | 4 | (5) | (1) |
| Week 3 | 4 | 4 | 7 | 3 | 3 |
| Week 4 | 7 | 9 | 8 | (1) | 1 |

*Example 6*

*To compare cumulative performance against cumulative forecast* and the like period in the previous year.

|  | Year 2 | Year 3 Budget | Year 3 Actual | Actual +/− Budget | Actual +/− Year 2 |
|---|---|---|---|---|---|
| Week 1 | 2 | 3 | 7 | 4 | 5 |
| Week 2 | 7 | 12 | 11 | (1) | 4 |
| Week 3 | 11 | 16 | 18 | 2 | 7 |
| Week 4 | 18 | 25 | 26 | 1 | 8 |

*Example 7*

*To pinpoint variance against average.* Arrive at the average and compare each man against the average.

|  | *Actual* | | | | | *Variance* | | |
|---|---|---|---|---|---|---|---|---|
|  | Mr A | Mr B | Mr C | Total | Average | Mr A | Mr B | Mr C |
| Jan. | 2 | 3 | 7 | 12 | 4 | (2) | (1) | 3 |
| Feb. | 5 | 9 | 4 | 18 | 6 | (1) | 3 | (2) |
| Mar. | 4 | 4 | 7 | 15 | 5 | (1) | (1) | 2 |
| Apr. | 7 | 9 | 8 | 24 | 8 | (1) | 1 | — |
| Total | 18 | 25 | 26 | 69 | 23 | (5) | 2 | 3 |

*Example 8*

*To establish cumulative variance against the cumulative average.* Arrive at the average of cumulative performance and compare each man's performance against this.

|  | *Actual* | | | | | *Variance* | | |
|---|---|---|---|---|---|---|---|---|
|  | Mr A | Mr B | Mr C | Total | Average | Mr A | Mr B | Mr C |
| Jan. | 2 | 3 | 7 | 12 | 4 | (2) | (1) | 3 |
| Feb. | 7 | 12 | 11 | 30 | 10 | (3) | 2 | 1 |
| Mar. | 11 | 16 | 18 | 45 | 15 | (4) | 1 | 3 |
| Apr. | 18 | 25 | 26 | 69 | 23 | (5) | 2 | 3 |

*Example 9*

*To express parts as a percentage of the whole (vertical).* Each man's total taken as 100 per cent with the parts broken down as a percentage of the total.

|  | *Actual* | | | *Percentages* | | |
|---|---|---|---|---|---|---|
|  | Mr A | Mr B | Mr C | Mr A | Mr B | Mr C |
| Retail | 2 | 3 | 7 | 11 | 12 | 27 |
| Wholesale | 5 | 9 | 4 | 28 | 36 | 15 |
| Industrial | 4 | 4 | 7 | 22 | 16 | 27 |
| Direct consumer | 7 | 9 | 8 | 39 | 36 | 31 |
|  | 18 | 25 | 26 | 100 | 100 | 100 |

*Example 10*

*To express parts as a percentage of the whole (horizontal).*

|  | *Actual* | | | | *Percentages* | | | |
|---|---|---|---|---|---|---|---|---|
|  | Mr A | Mr B | Mr C | Total | Mr A | Mr B | Mr C | Total |
| Retail | 2 | 3 | 7 | 12 | 17 | 25 | 58 | 100 |
| Wholesale | 5 | 9 | 4 | 18 | 28 | 50 | 22 | 100 |
| Industrial | 4 | 4 | 7 | 15 | 27 | 27 | 46 | 100 |
| Direct consumer | 7 | 9 | 8 | 24 | 29 | 38 | 33 | 100 |

*Example 11*

*To compare progress against budget.* Budget and Actual expressed as a percentage of the annual budget with variance expressed as a percentage plus or minus the cumulative budget.

|  | Year 2 | Year 3 Budget | Year 3 Actual | Year 2 (%) | Year 3 Budget (%) | Year 3 as Actual % of Budget | % Variance against Budget |
|---|---|---|---|---|---|---|---|
| 1st quarter | 2 | 3 | 7 | 11 | 12 | 28 | 133 |
| 2nd quarter | 7 | 12 | 11 | 39 | 48 | 44 | (8) |
| 3rd quarter | 11 | 16 | 18 | 61 | 64 | 72 | 12 |
| 4th quarter | 18 | 25 | 26 | 100 | 100 | 104 | 4 |

*Example 12*

*To establish trends through moving annual totals.* At the end of each quarter, that quarter's total is added to the previous 12-month figure, and the same quarter the preceding year is deducted. The quarterly average is a division by 4 of the annual figure.

|  | *Quarterly Actual* Year | | | *Annual Annual Total* Year | | | *Quarterly Average* Year | | |
|---|---|---|---|---|---|---|---|---|---|
|  | 1 | 2 | 3 | 1 | 2 | 3 | 1 | 2 | 3 |
| 1st quarter | 2 | 3 | 7 | — | 19 | 29 |  | 4.75 | 7.25 |
| 2nd quarter | 5 | 9 | 4 | — | 23 | 24 |  | 5.75 | 6.00 |
| 3rd quarter | 4 | 4 | 7 | — | 23 | 27 |  | 5.75 | 6.25 |
| 4th quarter | 7 | 9 | 8 | 18 | 25 | 26 | 4.5 | 6.25 | 6.5 |

*Presenting the information*

Just as important as not giving too much information is the need to present it as clearly as possible. A sales manager or others to whom we are providing information cannot act efficiently as a leader, motivator, trainer or controller if he is not supplied with the information on which he can act, presented to him by his sales office in a clear, readable, easily assimilable form.

*Form design*

Form design is very important, and care over this should extend a lot further than worrying only about the form used for presenting the final information to management. The forms sent to representatives, used by the accounts division, used by the warehouse and so on should all be carefully designed to ensure that their information is readily obtainable by the person who, in turn, has to record data from them.

The following hints will help in designing new forms:

1  First list all the information required.
2  Consult everyone concerned, about the range of information and its presentation.
3  Examine other forms to see if they can be adapted to take extra information needed.
4  Rough out alternative designs and get someone else to give their opinion, especially people who will use the form.
5  Make sure it will be the right size — not too big to file or photocopy, not awkward to fold and post — and remember to allow a blank margin all around it (for clarity, notation, binding, stapling etc.).
6  Leave enough space for the information asked for, and test the rough design by filling it in with real information (maybe use it for a while in 'mock' form before printing).
7  Make sure that you are not about to duplicate a lot of information already gathered on another form.
8  Make sure the working and instructions are perfectly clear for everyone who will have to use it.
9  Design it with all users in mind. Some forms are wrongly spaced for typewritten entries, and some have so many copies that they can only be filled in by pressing very hard with a ballpoint pen.
10  If the form takes a lot of data from other forms, or from a computer print-out, for instance, ensure that the entries will be in the same sequence.

*Illustrations*

Illustrations can put across some types of information a lot more easily than columns of figures. They can be particularly useful in summaries or to stress certain points, and a sales office is often called on to produce visually interesting material for sales conferences, sales meetings, board meetings and so on.

Frequently information that would otherwise be ignored can 'get across' with imaginative presentation. For example, one sales office, concerned at the high discounts the sales force was giving, produced a simple 'discount calculator' disc which showed at a glance how many more sales a representative would have to make to recover revenue lost by giving different discounts (see Figure 6.1).

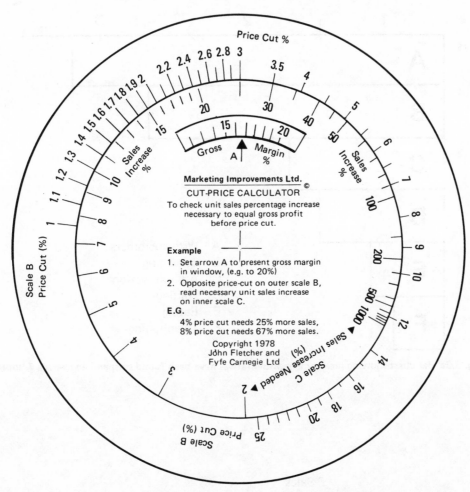

**Fig. 6.1 Creative visual presentation of figures — a discount calculator for salesmen**

This method could also be used to show the effect of price cuts, over high trade-ins, too long a credit period, and so on. Such information issued only as a plain sheet of figures would make little impact.

*Charts and graphs*

When it is important that trends and variance are clearly shown, rather than exact figures, it can be far better to use graphic representations of the data, rather than columns of figures which require a lot of mental effort to put in meaningful proportion and comparison. These are the most common ways of presenting data with visual emphasis:

*Bar charts* are used for representing 'class data', such as different activities over a given period of time (see Figure 6.2).

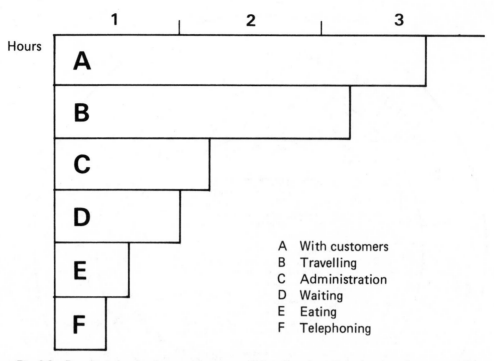

A    With customers
B    Travelling
C    Administration
D    Waiting
E    Eating
F    Telephoning

**Fig. 6.2a  Bar chart showing how some representatives have been found to spend an average 7-hour day**

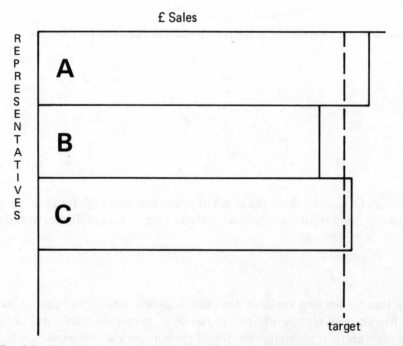

**Fig. 6.2b  Bar chart showing half-year comparison of representatives' progress towards targets**

*Pie charts* are also used for representation of class data (see Figure 6.3).

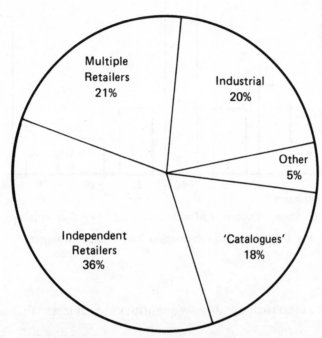

**Fig. 6.3  Pie chart comparing customer mix (by order volume) of customer selling 'gift' product (Fig. 6.2a could also equally well be shown as a pie chart).**

*Histograms* can be used for showing how quantities differ over time, or any other representation of 'frequency distribution' (see Figure 6.4).

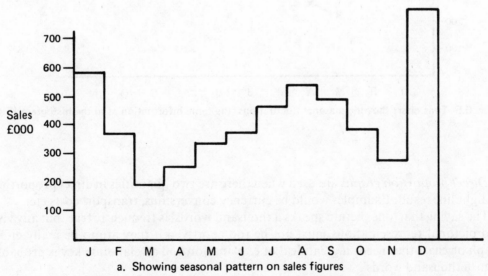

a.  Showing seasonal pattern on sales figures

**Fig. 6.4   Presenting information from figures: histogram·**

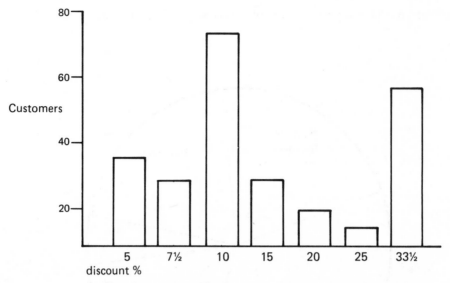

b. Showing numbers of orders given different discounts over a year

**Fig. 6.4  Presenting information from figures: histogram**

*Time charts* can be used to illustrate how quantities are subject to fluctuations over time (see Figure 6.5)

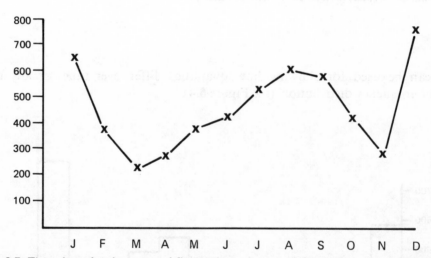

**Fig. 6.5  Time chart showing seasonal fluctuations, the same information as in the histogram (Fig. 6.4a)**

*Direct proportion graphs* are used when there are two quantities in direct proportion, and a straight line result. Examples would be currency conversions, transport costs etc.

The saying that 'one picture speaks a thousand words' is frequently true, but any visual aids and pictorial representations must not be too contrived if they are to be really effective. A graph or chart that needs a great deal of explanation and an elaborate key is probably worse than 'a thousand words'.

*Management by exception*

Managers who are determined not to be swamped by paperwork and irrelevant information frequently opt for 'management by exception'. This means simply the concept of dealing only with points likely to need acting upon rather than looking at all the information on everything. Instructions can be given that nothing is reported unless it is outside a certain fixed tolerance, or a few key factors can be chosen for regular scrutiny; other information is then only necessary when something does not go according to plan, and when standards are not met or are exceeded (we may be just as interested in discovering why results are better than we planned).

Management by exception has many uses in the sales office, consider the following.

*Budgetary control.* A line by line or total variance factor (plus or minus) can be set, and only items exceeding these variances are brought to management's attention.

*Performance levels.* These are particularly applicable to such factors as representatives' calling rates; i.e. if the target is 8 calls a day, an averaged variance of 2 over the month, plus or minus, might be regarded as an exception.

*Communication failures.* When action or information is requested, but not given, the sales manager is included in the second, follow-up request.

*Stock and sales levels.* Underline or extract only the exceptions on unit sales and stock level lists to save management having to look at lengthy statistical documents.

*Queries/complaints.* In most offices queries or complaints (and most companies get at least a few) come in at a fairly consistent level, but there may be increases due to seasons, problems with a new product or system. It is simple to record and classify queries, drawing management's attention if they increase by perhaps more than 10 per cent.

*Reports.* Many field reports can be reduced to a series of ticks in columns by asking specific questions. Variances can be quickly pinpointed.

*Summary*

In its supporting role to sales management and the marketing operation, the sales office should sift and pinpoint information. Sales management does not want to know when results are according to plan — it is the variance or the unusual that really needs attention.

Variance can be positive or negative, better than the plan or worse. A negative variance, however, may indicate a positive result, e.g. lower expenditure resulting in a cost saving.

# Part Three

# Increasing Sales

# 7:                                     *The Sales Approach*

Although the sales office plays mainly a supporting role to the sales force itself, it can often have a direct effect on sales and can therefore directly and immediately affect the company's profitability. There are four main areas where the sales office has this direct effect:

1   Via the company image.
2   Through response activity.
3   Through initiated activities.
4   Through support activities.

Before these areas can be looked at in detail, it is best to gain a proper understanding of the sales process and to appreciate what happens in a sale because such an understanding underlies all successful customer contact. There may also be special techniques some members of the sales office will have to learn. The meaning and implications of selling and of buying have to be understood before we can try to improve them.

 *The selling sequence*

The salesman who does not understand a buyer has a hard job selling anything, and the selling sequence cannot be followed or appreciated properly without understanding the buying process. We cannot sell without understanding how and why people buy. In the sales office, where almost all outside contact is with people who are at some stage of the buying process, this understanding of buying is very important.

Many staff who run a sales office come from an administrative rather than selling background, and as a result there is often an element of apprehension about having a selling role. But by understanding the buying process, and seeing its connection with selling, we can see the beliefs about selling ability are frequently myths, and that magical talents are not needed in order to be a satisfactory seller.

The process of selling cannot take place without communication, and that requires two people — the buyer and the seller. As in all communications, little is achieved if one does not understand the other. Let us therefore look at the buyer.

The buying process, which governs the buyer, can be broken down into seven stages through which the buying mind goes on its way to reach a decision. These stages are the following:

1  I am important and I want to be respected.
2  Consider my needs.
3  Now will your ideas help me?
4  What are the facts?
5  What are the snags?
6  What shall I do?
7  I approve.

Any sales attempt which responds unsatisfactorily to any of these stages is unlikely to end in an order. The buying mind has to be satisfied on each point before moving to the next, and to be successful a sales presentation sequence must match the buying sequence, and run parallel to it.

Figure 7.1 shows the buying process alongside the sales objectives, what we are trying to achieve at each stage, and the technique areas employed in any sales communication. The two keys to success are the process of matching the buyer's progression and describing, selectively, the product and discussing it in a way that relates to precisely what the buyer needs. This may be a little different to the way 'product knowledge' is generally organised for us, and is therefore examined in the next section.

| How people buy | | Sales objective | How to sell | Sales technique |
|---|---|---|---|---|
| 1 | I am important | To explore and identify customer's needs | | Opening the sales interview |
| 2 | Consider my needs | | | |
| 3 | How will your ideas help me? | To select and present the benefits which satisfy the customer's needs | | The sales presentation |
| 4 | What are the facts? | | | |
| 5 | What are the snags? | To prevent by anticipating snags likely to arise or handle objections raised so that the customer is satisfied with the answers | | Handling sales objections |
| 6 | What shall I do? | To obtain a buying decision from the customer or a commitment to the proposition presented to him | | Closing the sale |
| 7 | I approve | | | |

Fig. 7.1  The buying sequence

In all successful sales the buyer and the seller would have gone through this sequence stage by stage. If the attempt to sell (which just as often begins with an attempt to buy) is unsuccessful, it will be found that (a) the sequence has not taken place at all; (b) some stage or stages have been missed out; (c) the sequence has been followed too quickly or too slowly, which means the representative has allowed it to get out of step with the buying process.

In the sales office we may not always be able to aim for a commitment to buy, but we must have a clear objective on which to 'close' in mind. This may be to get the customer to allow us to send literature, to fix an appointment for a representative to call or to provide sufficient information for a detailed quotation to be prepared (though often there may be more opportunities to sell to the point of order than we realise, as we shall see later on, particularly looking at telephone selling). Whatever our objective is, however, it is important to know and be able to recognise the various stages ahead. With any customer contact (by telephone or letter as well as face to face) we can identify:

1　What stage has been reached in the buying process.
2　Whether our selling sequence matches it.
3　If not, why not?
4　What do we need to do if the sequence does not match?
5　Has a step been missed?
6　Are we going too fast?
7　Should we go back in the sequence?
8　Can our objectives still be achieved, or were they the wrong objectives?
9　How can we help the buyer through the rest of the buying process?

Naturally the whole buying process is not always covered in only one contact between company and customer. Every phone call does not result in a sale, and neither does it result in a lost sale. Some stages of the selling sequence have to be followed in each sales contact, but the logic applies equally to a series of calls which form the whole sales approach to each customer. For a doubtful customer, or a sale of great complexity and expense, there may be numerous contacts on just one of the stages before the buyer is satisfied and both can move on to the next stage:

Each call or contact has a selling sequence of its own in reaching the *call objectives*. Each call is a part of an overall selling sequence aimed at reaching *overall sales objectives*.

Planning the selling sequence is as much a part of call planning as it is of sales planning, but only rarely does a call take place exactly as planned. Knowing and using the sales sequence, and being able to recognise stages of the buying process, are invaluable if we are to realise the potential for direct sales results that the sales office has — if it is able to deal effectively with all calls, and pass on effectively those that will be completed by others in the organisation, e.g. salesman.

With this basic appreciation of the buyer, and what is directing his reactions, we can look closer at the key areas of the sales approach.

### *Using product information effectively*

Identifying with the buyer, in order to recognise the stages of the buying process and to match them with a parallel selling sequence, must extend into the presentation of the sales proposition. Nowhere is this more important than in the way we look at the product, or service, which we are selling.

Product knowledge is too often taken for granted by companies and salesmen. Sadly, experience of hearing hundreds of salesmen talking unintelligible gibberish does not support this complacency. Salesmen are usually given inadequate product knowledge and what is given is slanted towards the company and not the customer. Sales office staff are often even less well briefed. Managers are often still heard to say proudly, 'Everyone joining us spends six months in the factory, to learn the business', but many then emerge with no better idea of what the product means to the customer. Everyone with any role to play in sales-orientated customer contact must consider the product — and all that goes with it — from the customer's point of view.

*Don't sell products — sell benefits*

If we get into the habit of seeing things through the customer's eyes, we shall realise that we do not sell special promotions, 'free' trial offers or fancy wrappings. We do not really sell products either. We sell what customers want to buy and

CUSTOMERS DON'T BUY PROMOTIONS OR PRODUCTS — THEY BUY *BENEFITS*

*What are benefits?*

Benefits are what products, promotions or services do for the customer. It is not important what the products *are*, but *what they do or mean for the customer.*

A person does not buy an electric drill because he wants an electric drill, but because he wants to be able to make holes. He buys holes, not a drill. He buys the drill for what it will do (make holes) and this in turn may only be important to him because of a need for storage and a request to put up shelving.

Realising this not only makes selling more effective but also easier. We do not have to try to sell the same product to a lot of different people, but we meet each person's needs with personal benefits.

Benefits are what the things we sell can do for each individual customer — the things *he* wants them to do for *him*. Different customers buy the same product for different reasons. Therefore we must identify and use the particular benefits of interest to them.

What a product 'is' is represented by its 'features'.

What a product 'does' is described by its 'benefits'.

If this is forgotten, then the things which are important to a customer will not always be seen as important from the salesman's viewpoint, particularly if he has had little or no sales training. The result can, understandably, end up in the conflict of priorities shown in Figure 7.2.

| Customer | Salesman |
|---|---|
| 1 *Himself*<br>Satisfaction of his needs, e.g. mortgage to buy a house, new machine to increase production | 1 *Himself*<br>His company<br>His products<br>His ideas |
| 2 *His needs* and the benefits which satisfy them | 2 *His product* and making this customer buy it |
| 3 *This salesman*<br>Salesman's company<br>Salesman's products<br>Salesman's ideas | 3 *Benefits* to this customer |
| 4 *Buying* from this salesman | 4 *Customer's needs*<br>Benefits which satisfy this customer's needs |

Fig. 7.2  Differing viewpoints of salesman/customer

The customer is most unlikely to see things from the salesman's point of view. Everyone is to himself the most important person in the world. Therefore, to be successful, the salesmen has to be able to see things from the customer's point of view and demonstrate through his words and actions that he has done so. His chances of success are greater if he can understand the needs of the people he talks to and make them realise that he can help them fulfil those needs.

We achieve this essentially by the correct use of benefits. In *presenting any proposition to a customer, even simply recommending a product in reply to a query, we should always translate what we are offering into what it will do.*

Often a company — and the people who write the sales literature — grow product-orientated, and gradual product development can reinforce this attitude by adding more and more features. It is only a small step before everyone is busy trying to sell the product on its features alone. It is interesting to note that often when this happens advertising and selling become more and more forceful, with the features being given a frantic push, as passing time reveals that there has been no great rush to buy.

Two examples over the past years familiar to everyone are the audio and camera markets. Stereo equipment especially is almost always promoted only on features. Masses of technical terms, most of them meaningless to the majority of end-users, dominate advertisements and brochures, and the visual communication in them is based entirely on the appearance of the amplifier, speakers or turntable. Yet what people want from a stereo set is sound and reliability — years of listening pleasure.

When competitive products become almost identical in their performance, it can be difficult to sell benefits, since all seem to offer the same benefits. Choice then often depends on the personal appeal of some secondary feature. But even then, there must be emphasis on the benefits in those features, rather than on the features themselves. In 'industrial' selling (to other companies rather than to individual consumers) it is more important than ever to concentrate on benefits rather than on features, which may be little better than gimmicks. Features are only important if they support benefits that the customer is interested in.

Deciding to concentrate on benefits is only half the battle, however. They have to be the right benefits. In fact, benefits are only important to a customer if they describe the satisfaction of his needs. Working out the needs, and then the benefits, means being 'in the customers' shoes'.

## Who is the customer — what are his needs?

To know what benefits to put forward, we must know what the customers' needs are, and to know them we have to know exactly who the customer is. Very often the customer we deal with is the user — the person who will actually use the product. But frequently the direct customer is a purchaser or a decision-maker, who is not the user. This is most common in industrial selling, when a buying department is often responsible for ordering as well as handling the purchasing for most of a company's requirements. In consumer products a manufacturer may sell to a wholesaler, the wholesaler to a retailer, and it is only the retailer who actually sells to the user.

Naturally the requirements of the end-user will also be of interest to the various intermediaries, but the best results are going to be obtained if we can bear in mind the needs of both the buyer and the user, and the differences between their various needs.

To do this, it is convenient to use a product feature/benefit analysis, which also helps to differentiate between features and benefits. An example of this process is shown in Figure 7.3. Such analysis can be produced for each product, or for a product range, and is perhaps particularly useful for new products. Again this is an exercise that can be shown within an office, or section, to spread the task and help everyone learn just what is a feature and a benefit.

Note that not all the needs will be objective ones; most buyers, including industrial ones, also have subjective requirements bound up in their decisions. The graph in Figure 7.4 illustrates this concept: the line does not touch either axis as no product is bought on an entirely objective or subjective basis. Sometimes even with technical products the final decision can be heavily influenced by subjective factors, perhaps seemingly of minor significance, once all the objective needs have been met.

By matching benefits to individual customer needs, we are more likely to make a sale, for a

| Customer needs | Benefits that will satisfy customer needs | Product features from which the benefits are derived |
|---|---|---|
| **1 Rational** | | |
| *Performance* — must be able to work fast with a variety of implements | Plenty of power, particularly at low speeds | A 65 BHP diesel engine with high torque at low rpm. Wide range of matched implements available |
| *Versatility* — must cope with a variety of soil and cultivating conditions | Can travel at a wide variety of speeds | A 10-speed synchromesh gearbox — four wheel drive available for very difficult conditions |
| *Simplicity* — must be easy to operate | Simple and speedy implement changeover. Easy to drive | Quick-attach linkage with snap-on hydraulic couplings. Ergonomically placed levers and pedals |
| *Low cost* — must be economical to run | Low fuel consumption | Efficient engine design with improved braking and fuel injector system. Good power/weight ratio |
| *Reliability* — must be able to operate continuously and be serviced quickly | Well-proven design with all basic snags removed. Local dealer with 24 hour parts service | More than 10000 units already in operation. Wide dealer network with factory-trained mechanics backed by computerised parts operation |
| **2 Emotional** | | |
| *Security* — (fear of making wrong decision) | Most popular tractor on the market — 10000 farmers can't be wrong | Largest company in the industry with good reputation for reliability and value for money |
| *Prestige* — (desire to gain status in the eyes of others) | Chosen by those engaged in best agricultural practice | Favoured by agricultural colleges and large farmers |

**Notes**

1 The product analysis should be completed from left to right. Only when the needs have been identified can the appropriate benefits and the relevant features be selected.

2 If the salesman works from right to left not only will he lose his buyer's interest as he talks about items which may not be of interest, but also he will have no basis for selecting which benefits to stress.

3 This example is not intended as a complete analysis. That can only be done with a specific buyer in mind as each person has an individual need pattern. Performance will be most important to one farmer, low cost to another.

4 It will be noted that some of the product features are so technical as to be almost meaningless to the layman. This is one of the greatest dangers for the industrial salesman. Unless he translates his trade jargon he will fail to achieve understanding and thus cannot be persuasive.

**Fig. 7.3  Product feature/benefit analysis (agricultural tractor example)**

(This chart is taken from *Training Salesmen on the Job* by John Lidstone, of Marketing Improvements Limited)

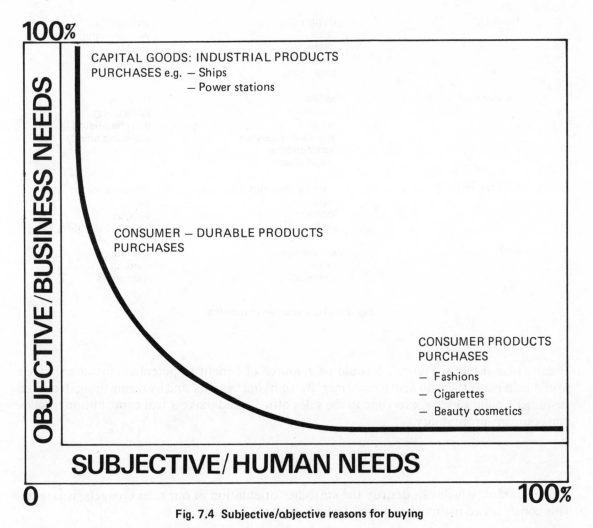

Fig. 7.4 Subjective/objective reasons for buying

product's benefits must match a buyer's needs. The features are only what give a product the right benefits.

By going through this process for particular products, and for segments of the range, and matching the factors identified to customer *needs*, a complete 'databank' of product information *from the customer's viewpoint* can be organised.

### Using the benefit approach

The sales office does not only sell and help sell products, it is uniquely positioned to promote services and the company as a whole. With competitive products becoming increasingly similar, more buyers quickly conclude that their main needs can be met by more than one product. Other needs then become more important. If, for instance, a buyer needs a crane, he is likely to find a number of them which will lift the weight required, and which will all cost practically the same.

The deciding factors will then become availability, service and repair facilities, and so on.

In the sales office we can look at the 'features' contained by the company as a whole, and be ready to convert them to benefits to customers — in the same way as we can practise finding benefits for the full product range. The aspects, shown in Figure 7.5 (and others), are all sources of benefits to customers.

| Products | design | storage |
|---|---|---|
| | price | workmanship |
| | delivery | credit |
| | appearance | stocks |
| | packaging | |
| Services | speed | training |
| | availability | advertising |
| | credit | merchandising |
| | after-sales service | pre-sales advice |
| | maintenance | |
| | installation | |
| Companies | time established | labour relations |
| | reputation | size |
| | location | policies |
| | philosophy | financial standing |
| Staff | knowledge | availability |
| | skill | training |
| | character | specialists |

Fig. 7.5  Four sources of benefits

Each item listed in Figure 7.5 could be a source of benefit to potential customers which would help make them an actual customer. By 'thinking benefits' and by seeing things from the customer's point of view, everyone in the sales office could make a real contribution to sales and company profitability.

*Jargon*

A final hazard, which can destroy the customer orientation of our sales contacts, is jargon. This comes in two main forms, both of which can confuse customers:

1   *Technical or industrial jargon.* We should always let the customer be first to use it. Technological complexities have already led to thousands of new words and phrases in business and industry, and introducing still more new terms seldom helps. But worst of all is the possibility that the customer will not know what we are talking about, or will form the wrong impression, yet will hesitate to admit it.

2   *Company jargon.* It is even more important to avoid company jargon, for here the customer will be on very unfamiliar ground. There is a world of difference between 'We'll do a sales/stock return compo and the computer chappie will feed in to the fourth floor, so we can let you know very shortly', and 'To answer your query we'll have to do a comparison of the sales and stock return movements. The quickest way will be to ask for a computer print-out which Head Office will forward to us. I will contact you with the answer in a week or ten days time'.

    Company jargon can affect everything we deal with, and even simple phrases can cause trouble. For example, delivery is one area for potential misunderstanding. Promising 'immediate delivery' might, in our terms, mean getting the product to the customer within a week, for normal delivery might take 3 weeks. But what if the customer is in the pharmaceutical industry, where 'immediate delivery' is jargon for 'within eight hours'? He is almost bound to get the wrong impression.

Knowing how and why customers buy is a prerequisite to improving all the specific contact areas examined next.

# 8: Company Image

Every company has an image. Will it be positive? What sort of impact will it make in the market? It cannot be seen, touched, described, wrapped up and sold; nor can a company simply go out and 'buy' an instant image. An image cannot be replenished from a storeroom, but it can run down; and because it is not a physical thing that can be checked, the company itself is very often the last to realise that its image is low or is declining.

A company's image, however, is very important and deserves practically as much attention as the product or service that the company sells. A bad image can do almost as much damage to a company's profits as a bad product or an inferior service can.

Even a good product can have its sales spoilt by a bad company image — it will be so much more difficult for a customer, prejudiced by the company's bad image, to believe that the product will perform as claimed. The long-term effect of a bad image can be disastrous. If customers find it unpleasant dealing with a company over a period, they will begin to suspect the product, especially if they cannot pinpoint exactly what makes them uneasy with the company, which is the usual consequence of a bad image. Even if there has been no change in the product, it will be 'felt' to be getting worse.

Not only can old customers be lost in that way but new customers are seldom gained. Reputation and word of mouth comments spread rapidly, and have more impact than the most expensive advertising. A bad company image spreads — and sticks.

### Influences on an image

A company gets its image from the impression it creates on the public in general, and on its customers and potential customers in particular. To them, a company *is* what they happen to see and experience. Thus everything and everyone that can come into contact with customers and the public can influence the company image, and so have an effect on sales and profitability.

A company whose dirty delivery vans are driven with no consideration for others by men wearing any old tatty clothes, and which sends out incorrect statements, answers letters belatedly and on unattractive, dull letterheads (using obviously ancient and ill-serviced typewriters), and has an inefficient, rude switchboard, and so on, will develop such a bad company image that it can be doomed to gradual extinction, no matter how excellent its product. A company attracts the staff and customers it deserves. A bad company gradually gets a poor staff and fewer and fewer customers, which means that more staff leave, to be replaced by even worse staff, which worsens the image yet further ...

## Improving the image

Obviously a good image is essential, and obviously the sales staff, so frequently in direct or indirect contact with customers, has a major influence on company image. The sales office manager may actively have to try to influence the other divisions in the company, which also affect the image, apart from seeing to his own staff.

Let us look first at two positions in the company which, because they usually have first contact with outsiders, can be as important for the company's image as the longer contact between customer and sales office. These are the telephone switchboard and the receptionist.

### The telephone switchboard

When was the last time you telephoned your own organisation, without it being immediately clear who you were? How did the experience leave you feeling? Satisfied, pleased or perhaps dismayed? If you have not done this recently, do so soon; it could be very informative.

On every incoming call, the telephonist is the first person a customer or prospective customer speaks to. The impression she gives is vitally important, and deserves far more attention than many companies give. In some companies the telephonist is under the direct responsibility of the sales office, but usually the sales office manager will have to be diplomatic about suggesting improvements to whoever they report to — perhaps the personnel/administration manager. The fact that the majority of incoming calls are probably destined for 'somewhere in sales' is sufficient justification for the sales division to 'interfere' (in the best sense) in someone else's area.

A desultory mumbling of the telephone number (eventually) by way of a greeting, and then an excellent chance of being misrouted or left in a silent telephone limbo, are telephone techniques that we have all come across too often. Given the choice, we try — as customers — never to repeat them. We take our business elsewhere.

A good telephonist answers promptly and politely — an overworked switchboard is no excuse for delay or rudeness and more money will go on lost business than on recruiting another telephonist. Greetings should be short, friendly, informative: '5943' is not suitable, even if said with a question mark. 'Hello' is equally useless and impolite, for it invariably puts the onus on the caller to ask, 'Is that Country Caravans?'.

'Good Morning, Country Caravans ... may I help you?', said with a reasonable amount of enthusiasm, is well worth the trouble. The telephonists who do this and their other tasks properly are valuable members of their companies, to be paid accordingly.

If the telephonist is required to ask the caller's name, she should be sure to use it when she puts the call through, e.g. 'Mr Smith, I am putting you through to Mr Brown now'. But it is pointless to do that if what happens next is that a phone rings on Mr Brown's desk, and Brown has to establish for himself who is calling. If the telephonist has discovered the name, she should phone Brown and say, 'Mr Smith is on the line for you, Mr Brown', before connecting them.

The good telephonist does not keep callers waiting, especially in silence. Some callers cannot hear if phone extensions are ringing; for all they know they have been forgotten, and 'Brown' has not been tried yet. Calls are expensive. If the person being called does not answer or cannot take the call, the message should be, 'I am sorry Mr Smith, but Mr Brown is not available — may I take a message?'.

If Brown is being called to the phone, the telephonist should speak to the caller frequently to reassure him, to apologise for his wait, and to give him the opportunity to leave a message and ring off. Messages must be taken down carefully and accurately.

A message pad tailored to your particular company, printed (with, if necessary, carbon copies) and on a standard size paper, perhaps A4, not only ensures messages are taken clearly, it puts an added importance on them and often removes the necessity for transcribing, as the resulting sheet can be neatly added to correspondence, a customer file and so on. Very few customer enquiries have to go astray for the extra trouble of preparing such a form to be worth while. The example used in Figure 3.7 is constructed on these principles. There is no reason why a different form from others in the company cannot be used in and on behalf of the sales office.

The good telephonist treats the caller with consideration. If the caller asks for a person by name, he should be put straight through unless specific instructions have been left for certain calls to be re-routed. The telephonist should know all names and functions (the internal directory should be sufficiently detailed) and know enough about the company's affairs to avoid the re-transferring of calls.

In companies where other divisions also have heavy telephone traffic, a separate number and switchboard is sometimes used for the sales and order departments. Then there is no excuse for a bad telephone technique causing a bad image, since it will be under the sales office manager's direct control.

In the next chapter we see how the telephone can be used to great advantage by the sales office in furthering sales. First, however, it is important to realise that impressions about the company are formed in numerous ways, and that many people gain their impression over the telephone. Everyone who uses it, and the switchboard operator most of all, should appreciate that courtesy and consideration cost nothing.

There are of course problems when the switchboard is not controlled by the sales office. (Perhaps it should be? Perhaps that is possible?) Even so, the sales office can make itself responsible for briefing the switchboard as to how their calls should be handled. Even difficult problems can be overcome if this is tackled correctly.

Let us say that the manager of a sales department asks his secretary to raise the question of service received from the switchboard with the manager to whom the operators report. Growth in the sales department has been followed by a deterioration of service.

One approach is to complain of the service, asking for — or demanding — better, maybe priority, service. This may start by producing a defensive reaction and make things more difficult.

Another is to form some plan of action first, and sell this as an advantage to the switchboard and its manager. Thus:

> We seem to be causing some problems to the switchboard, and have no wish to disrupt their normally efficient service.
> We have devised a scheme to make servicing our calls easier.

Then the idea is presented — maybe a visual chart and sequence of questions to make sure the operator puts calls through correctly. This will need to be presented in such a way as to 'sell' the benefits to the manager, and should attempt to anticipate any objections, and suggest specific action: for example, 'Can I discuss this with the supervisor and implement it immediately?' Such an approach will stand a better chance than a complaint of getting an improvement and satisfying both parties.

*Reception*

Just as important for its 'first image' responsibility is the role of reception, particularly if there is an associated showroom, or demonstration facility. As obvious as this may sound, many companies still greet customers and strangers with a cold, bare room, one stained table and a broken ashtray for furniture, yesterday's newspaper or an out-of-date price list for reading, and a frosted glass panel with a bell push and 'ring for attention' by way of a greeting. Only slightly better than the unfriendly sliding panel is the presence of a totally bored school leaver, who takes an age to look up from her magazine, knitting, or nail polish to mutter 'Yes?'

The reception area and the receptionist, the switchboard operator, the company letterhead, the vans, the packaging and labels — these are all opportunities to advertise the company. The image they portray is the image people have of the whole company.

The receptionist should greet callers in the same manner as the telephonist should, adding a personable, cheerful countenance. She should have an up-to-date list of everyone in the company, know where to direct callers, who to contact by telephone and how to handle impatient people.

A very common fault is to give the receptionist nothing else to do but receive, which means that often she has nothing to do at all. A caller who finds a receptionist reading, knitting, or gazing blankly into space, or sees her doing so while he waits for an appointment, can hardly think of the company as being dynamic and thriving.

Appearance is as important as attitude, which means that the receptionist should be smartly dressed and that the whole reception area should have a clean, pleasant appearance. It should never be used as a 'goods inwards' department, and other staff should only be in the area if they are meeting a visitor, not conducting an internal argument about product quality or management attitudes.

The reception area should be a silent salesman. In addition to the company's advertising materials, samples of the product (perhaps suitably annotated if it is technical) or a series of visually appealing company-orientated photographs can be on display. The reception area is also an ideal place to exhibit company awards, certificates, letters of commendation etc.

Unexpected visitors should always be seen by someone from the department concerned, if not by the very person the visitor came to see — even if it is only to explain to the visitor that an appointment is essential, and to agree a time for an appointment. If a customer's enquiry cannot be dealt with fully, a member of the sales staff should explain why, help the visitor as much as possible and provide him with all available literature, and ensure that an appointment is made when the customer will be able to get what he requires.

If it is unavoidable to keep visitors waiting for any length of time, it creates a far better impression if someone from the office, rather than the receptionist, comes to tell the visitor that he will have to wait, offers a cup of tea or coffee, something to read, and perhaps explores his needs to help brief whoever will subsequently see him. Be honest about time: do not say it will only be 10 minutes' wait when you know full well it will be half an hour. This only guarantees 20 minutes of annoyance.

Anyone calling on a company begins forming an impression the moment the building is seen. A customer, even if only subconsciously, will be wondering 'Will this company satisfy my needs?'. Since no one likes to be kept waiting, the reception area can become a most critical place for lost sales. Everything the company does in its contacts with callers should try to answer the customer's query with 'Yes, this company *is* likely to satisfy my needs'.

### *Individual attitudes of the sales staff*

The sales office is usually the first department with which a new customer has contact, and very often it is not a salesman or someone with special sales training who provides that first contact. Telephone enquiries, or calls in person, are frequently dealt with by someone in the sales office.

Every member of the staff must recognise that the first essential in making a sale is to gain the confidence of the buyer. Later on in the book we shall look at the importance of motivating the sales staff, but this is one of the areas where motivation is vital, for what is needed is a constant positive attitude by everyone towards improving sales. This positive attitude should show itself in numerous ways.

### *Interest*

It is hard for a customer to maintain interest in the face of indifference. Enthusiasm is infectious. Customers should get the impression that the company is glad to be in contact with them — helping customers is the reason for the company being in business, and not the tiresome interruptions which some companies seem to think it is. Sales staff should listen to customers' problems, ask questions about applications of products, satisfaction with service, and so on. A customer who feels that a company is not only interested in his money will always go back, and even higher prices are unlikely to shift his allegiance.

### *Courtesy*

In all circumstances, staff should try to stay polite and calm, however severe the aggravation. If a customer complains, apologise sincerely and do not attach qualifications or excuses to the apology. The normal reaction is to 'fight back', but the person who keeps cool invariably emerges the winner. An unreserved apology costs nothing, and it is the best way to deflate an irate complainer; besides, there is often more to the matter than is assumed at initial contact. Turning away customers who arrive just on closing time, or putting on an act of devastating self-sacrifice to postpone lunch by two minutes does nothing to enhance the company's image.

### *Efficiency*

Enquiries and queries should be dealt with quickly and effectively, even if it only means that the customer has to be contacted to be informed of a delay. But we should never commit ourselves to a particular course of action without first checking that it can be fulfilled. Never make promises unless they can be kept! Personal promises, however lightly given and seemingly unimportant, must always be honoured: a promise to phone back with some information should be kept even if the information cannot be obtained as quickly as expected.

It is another case of putting ourselves in the customer's shoes, and imagining what he expects us to do — then doing it.

### *Loyalty*

However tempting it may be to blame another person in the company or another department when we are facing the consequence of their own inefficiency or mistakes, we should always try to back the company. There is always a way of telling the customer that not everyone in the company is efficient without saying something like, 'Oh, I agree with you — you've no idea what it is like working in this madhouse', or '... not those idiots in dispatch again'. Do not belittle the customer's contact with us, and the individual with whom he deals, with phrases like 'Mr Jones is never here during the day, he is only a salesman'. Seeing things from the customer's viewpoint does not mean joining him in an alliance against the company.

*Atmosphere*

This can be conveyed by appearances, by telephone or by letter. Try to create an atmosphere of authority and efficiency. Use department and job titles, and have phone calls answered (on behalf of the representatives) with 'Mr Smith's secretary speaking — may I help you?'. Remarks such as 'I'll get your area representative, Miss Cole, to contact you as soon as she returns', all help to improve the image of the company.

One neat example of overcoming a potential problem and expressing interest, efficiency and loyalty, was demonstrated by a useful idea I saw originally on a print representative's business card. It worked like this. The front of the card was conventional, listing his name, company address and other details. On the back was the name of his assistant in the sales office (who in fact undertook the same role for several salesmen) and his sales manager, with their contact details. This was used with a neat explanation: the salesman was usually away from the office — the customer might be concerned as to the progress of proofs etc. — in normal circumstances the sales office would know what was going on — any real problems do not hesitate to call the sales manager. This idea helps in a number of ways, and is probably good motivationally for the sales office personnel, to whom the right calls should be easily directed.

### Manning the sales office

It is no good going to great lengths to ensure that everyone in the sales office tries to convey an enthusiastic, efficient image if there is no one in it when customers phone or call. From the time the sales office opens in the morning until the time it closes at night, the telephone must be continuously manned; and if personal callers are a normal occurrence, there must be someone to deal with them. The customer cannot be expected to know when coffee breaks, lunch hours and tea breaks are taken.

Rotas should be established to ensure that there are always enough people on duty to take messages or to deal directly with the enquiries, even if this does mean that everyone who would like to do so cannot then have lunch together. There are still some companies that use an automatic machine to answer the telephone at lunchtime; but however politely the message is recorded, it will still mean 'Sorry our lunch is more important for the moment, try later'. Informative messages should be taken down accurately and staff returning from lunch, or other absences from the office, should immediately respond to the messages.

It is very important that those on the rota have the required skills to use the phone. The caller has already been baulked by not being able to speak to the person he wanted to; and having to deal with an uninterested, impolite and uninformed person is going to cause a lot more damage to the prospects of a sale.

### Correspondence

In the next chapter, Chapter 9, on Response Activities, we shall see how many opportunities there are for making sales letters more effective. But while every letter to a customer has something to do with the selling sequence, not all letters are 'selling' letters. That is no reason to treat them carelessly, however, for even the briefest letter on the most mundane matter can influence the image its receiver has of the company.

The company has probably been at pains to obtain a well-designed and attractive letterheading — part of the image it hopes to portray, and perhaps echoing a theme found on its invoices and statements, on its packaging, delivery vehicles, and so on. That effort is totally wasted if the letter below it is badly put, unattractively laid out and poorly typed.

The following can help make sure that the letter is worthy of the letterhead and enhances the company image:

1　Position the letter on the page according to the amount of the text. It is unattractive if there is a huge expanse of white below a very short letter. Position it lower down, in that case, or, better still, have two sizes of letterhead paper, and do short letters on the smaller sheets (they could also be used for handwritten compliment slips).

2　'Block' paragraphs, with double spacing between each paragraph for greater clarity and smartness.

3　Leave at least 1½ inches at the foot of the page before going on to page 2; leave a bigger space to avoid having only one or two lines (plus farewells) for the second page.

4　Allow enough space for the signature, name and job title; rather carry the letter over on to another page than cram it in at the bottom.

5　Note, at the foot of the last page, the enclosures mentioned in the text and sent with the letter.

6　Staple the pages together to avoid losses.

7　Number the pages.

8　Make sure the type faces are regularly cleaned.

9　Do not use worn typewriter ribbons — the small saving in cost is not worth it.

10　Number the paragraphs when a lot of points have to be covered.

11　Underline all headings.

12　Ensure that there is a standard maintained throughout the company.

13　Avoid jargon and long-winded sentences.

Remember layout cannot be simply left to the secretary or typist. How a letter is originated will also help precision and prevent retyping: e.g. state when dictating on to a tape how long the letter will be.

Letter composition can be simple, but it is common for people to imagine it as difficult and 'very important'. Consequently too much thought goes into the writing, half-forgotten phrases from out-of-date school exercise books are brought out, and an unnatural atmosphere of solemn responsibility overtakes the writer. The result is a stilted letter, at worst full of archaic phrases such as 'Further to your esteemed communication of the 15th ult'. A useful hint is to think what would be said directly to the customer or over the phone, and then write the letter as closely as possible to that.

When the letter is handwritten — and some long or important letters should always be done in draft form first — check it over, and perhaps, if it is a really important letter, have someone else read it before it is finally typed and posted. The points to run over when a draft letter is being checked are shown in Figure 8.1.

One last word on letters: it is very easy to lose track of elapsed time when dealing with written queries. It is so easy to put letters aside, unlike the intrusive, demanding telephone calls, or the physical presence of a customer. The chart in Figure 8.2 shows how quickly time — seen from the customer's viewpoint — can pass by if a written query is held up, and how easily the total query time can vary from 'acceptable' to 'far too long'. Certain factors, like the way things occur in relation to a weekend, or the precise method adopted for reply — letter (first- or

|  | YES | NO |
|---|---|---|
| 1   Is the letter written from the viewpoint of the person to whom it is addressed? | | |
| 2   Will the opening secure favourable attention? | | |
| 3   Does the letter cover all the information necessary to achieve its purpose? | | |
| 4   Are the statements in logical order? | | |
| 5   Are all parts of the proposition fully covered? | | |
| 6   Does the letter avoid or overcome objections? | | |
| 7   Is the request for response or action well expressed? | | |
| 8   Is the general appearance of the letter good? | | |
| 9   Is it grammatically correct? | | |
| 10   Is it properly punctuated? | | |
| 11   Is it logically paragraphed? | | |
| 12   Is it free from trite and poorly chosen expressions? | | |
| 13   Is it easy to read? | | |
| 14   Can it be improved by shortening? | | |
| 15   Are enclosures listed? (and included!) | | |

Fig. 8.1   Checkpoints for satisfactory letters

| | Alternative A | B | C | D |
|---|---|---|---|---|
| Mon. | 1 Posted | | 1 Posted | |
| Tue. | 2 In manager | | 2 In/Out manager | |
| Wed. | 3 Out manager | | 3 In/Out clerk | |
| Thur. | 4 In clerk | 1 Posted | 4 In/Out manager | 1 Posted |
| Fri. | 5 Out clerk | 2 In Manager | 5 Received | 2 In/Out manager In/Out clerk |
| Sat. | 6 | 3 | | 3 |
| Sun. | 7 | 4 | | 4 |
| Mon. | 8 In manager | 5 Out manager | | 5 In/Out manager |
| Tue. | 9 Out manager | 6 In clerk | | 6 Received |
| Wed. | 10 Received | 7 Out clerk | | |
| Thur. | | 8 In manager | | |
| Fri. | | 9 Out manager | | |
| Sat. | | 10 | | |
| Sun. | | 11 | | |
| Mon. | | 12 Received | | |

**Fig. 8.2 Examining time factors from the customer's viewpoint**

second-class post), telex, telephone — can have a marked effect. In the example shown the time varies from 5 to 12 days, with very little difference in the way action is taken.

The company image, then, can be as effective an order puller as an expensive advertising campaign or the steady work of an excellent field sales force. The work of the latter, too, can easily be undone by a bad image — and a bad image comes from laziness and an 'I don't care' attitude. A good image has to be worked for, and the sales office can do a great deal to generate a good company image — not least by example.

# 9: Response Activities

Response activities are those activities carried out by the sales office as a result of some outside 'stimulus'. Usually they are replies to customer and trade contacts and enquiries, which may have been by telephone, by letter or by someone calling in person. In many sales offices they account for a large percentage of the total work.

The nature of contact can vary. It may be a straightforward enquiry, such as asking for a price, querying availability or asking about some technical specification. Many will be direct, immediate orders, or will be the sort of enquiry which is the preliminary move in ordering, such as 'Do you have your 3 hp electric motor available for immediate delivery?' Some calls are bound to be complaints.

The way we respond will vary, too. Usually we will be able to answer most price and specification enquiries, unless they involve special conditions or combinations of products. We should be able to action most orders immediately. If there is anything that has to be passed on to others, this may still make it necessary for us to monitor or supervise the progress of the enquiry.

No matter what the eventual outcome of a call or enquiry is, we should always aim at the following:

1   To take action in such a way that we maximise the chances of making a sale, now or in the future (or both).
2   To do so within the organisational and cost parameters set by the company (we clearly cannot go personally to collect every prospect in the company Rolls and take him for lunch at the Ritz).

In order to achieve these aims, we need to employ (a) our knowledge of the company and its products (regarded specifically in the customer's terms), and (b) sales skills, often in special areas, such as are employed over the telephone and in letter writing.

No matter what the enquiry is or whether we can handle it in the sales office or have to pass it on to another person or division for progressing or completion, we should always be aware of two things — accuracy and timing.

*Accuracy*

Accuracy is naturally very important, and without it we have little chance of servicing any kind of customer enquiry correctly. Not only could we get the enquirer's name and address wrong, but we could incorrectly interpret his question, which would lead to the expense of having to change a wrong order or to a lost order or lost repeat orders.

Before responding to an enquiry we need to check the following:

1    Is the customer's product description (especially in a letter) clear, or could it be ambiguous? Are we absolutely sure we and the customer are talking about the same thing?
2    Have we got his name and address correctly over the telephone? Have we checked the spelling, especially of the caller's own name?
3    Have we added essential internal information, such as the enquirer's account number or credit rating?
4    Did we make a note of all the commitments or promises we made on the telephone?

One of the easiest ways to be certain that we are accurate is to have some formalisation in this area. Telephone message pads and enquiry forms are very useful aids; the former has already been illustrated (Figure 3.7), and an example of an enquiry form designed to progress, not just record, the enquiry is shown in Figure 9.1. It may help you design your own.

Such a form acts additionally as a checklist, prompting those using it to obtain information that will complete the picture, e.g. *Why* does the customer want the product? While it may not always be possible, indeed necessary, to complete all the form, everything beyond the basic information may help, i.e. increase the chances of a sale being ultimately made successfully.

*Timing*

Two important points about timing are the key to good customer service, for it is quite likely that there is more argument and dissatisfaction over time than about anything else. They are the following:

1    Be aware *how long things take from a customer's standpoint*. Simple analysis, which includes time in the post, time in the company's internal post, and time waiting in in-trays, can show surprising results. Look again at the examples in Figure 8.2. If speed of response is vital, we need to have some way of assessing costs of postage, telex, telephone etc. in the context of the situation or customer we are dealing with. A priority system could be introduced — all complaints requiring a written answer to use first-class post, certain overseas customers to have telex replies, and so on.
2    Be aware of *commitments on time*, so that if we promise to phone back at 3.30 p.m., or see that the customer has certain information tomorrow, then that is what must happen (and 24 hours late, even 30 minutes late, is not good enough). The customer *will* notice, and probably will be half expecting you to call back earlier. If a delay is going to be completely unavoidable, it is essential to contact the customer immediately to let him know, this can also prevent him feeling he has to telephone us himself to check or chase.

It is important to remember the strict criteria for accuracy and timing, and it is just as important to appreciate that there is more to response activities than merely a response. Every contact with a customer is an opportunity to move along, or initiate, the selling sequence.

To:          From:
Ref:   **№ 4819**

# Enquiry Progress Form

| | |
|---|---|
| Enquiry taken by:      Date: | Company: |
| | Address: |
| Source of enquiry: | |
| Stated need: | Tel No: |
| | Contact name: |
| | Position: |
| Comments: | Company by Product: |
| | Additional Information: |
| Action taken: | |
| Action promised (inc. timing): | |

Subsequent progress:

| Date | |
|---|---|
| | |

Resulting Order:  Value
Order Number      Date

**Fig. 9.1 Example of enquiry progress form**

With this in mind, we can look closely at the three major response activities which need to be handled correctly if we are not to lose customers, and which frequently offer opportunities for selling. These are (a) complaints, (b) sales letters, and (c) telephone calls. To get the negative one out of the way first, let us examine complaints.

## Complaints

Every company gets complaints — even the best run, with the best products and the best service. Many complaints are minor, but something serious inevitably happens from time to time. How we react and how we deal with customers will determine whether complaints lead to lost customers. We can perhaps even think of situations ourselves where a well-handled complaint leaves us almost more inclined to return to a supplier than if the complaint had never occurred. This is perhaps particularly true of services, for example, hotels. Serious complaints usually get lots of action, and paradoxically may not lose a customer as quickly as through a minor complaint — because minor complaints are often ignored, resulting in a customer who gets *more* dissatisfied as a result of complaining, instead of less.

Considering the amount of time, money and effort that goes into getting new customers, we should obviously take great care to keep the ones we have, and no complaint should ever be thought of as so minor that it can be totally ignored. It is usually up to the sales office staff to handle complaints, and it is the sales staff who can take the sting out of complaints and begin to turn a complaining customer into a satisfied customer ready to place another order.

Complaints are 'emotive', both with the customer and with the sales staff, and this must be taken into account. In order to make the complaint (something many people actually find difficult) the customer will often get more 'worked up' than is necessary, partly in anticipation of a defensive, argumentative attitude by the company. Our own reaction to criticism is also likely to make us over-react, especially since, in the sales office, we frequently have to answer for the actions of other departments and other individuals. We must take an impartial view, however, remaining loyal to the company and all employees, but above all providing satisfaction for the customer.

### What complaints mean

We always learn from mistakes, and we can also learn from complaints. They may, for instance, indicate problem areas within the company, and clearing up that problem area will make things run more smoothly, perhaps improving sales. One particular complaint may bring such a problem area to light for the first time, or it may only be apparent through analysis of complaints received over a period.

Clearly, we must look for the meaning behind complaints, as well as trying to satisfy the customer. There must, therefore, be a way of informing management about them, especially when a problem area rather than one-off mistakes is indicated.

The best way to do this is through complaint forms, which can be analysed by someone senior in the company, and action taken as necessary. It is far better for the system and for morale if this action is seen as being corrective rather than punitive. Complaint forms should not be viewed as black marks for some poor employee (unless a series of them indicate one employee's poor conduct) but as a system to correct faults.

The complaint form is another example of a form which should be tailored to an individual company requirement — one which should be sufficiently comprehensive to act as a checklist, or progressing system as well as a record. Again large size, A4, paper is recommended. An example appears in Figure 9.2.

To: _____    Copies to:  ☐ Production

_____                    ☐ Area Manager

                                             ☐ Representative

                                             ☐ _____

Taken by: _____    Date: _____    Time: _____

Complainant's Name: _____    Position: _____

Company: _____

Address: _____

_____

_____

Telephone Number: _____

Nature of complaint:

_____

_____

_____

_____

---

ACTION

Action taken:                            Action promised:

Follow-up action suggested:

**Fig. 9.2 Example of complaint form**

Complaints arise from the following:

1    Products.
2    Service functions.
3    Company policy and conduct.
4    Employee actions.
5    Factors outside the company's control.

Whether they are oral or written, there are only two 'types' of complaint: justified, and unjustified or mistaken. The information taken from the customer, whether or not a complaint form is used, should be sufficiently detailed to allow its 'type' to be identified, and provide a basis for prompt investigation, checking and answering the complaint, either immediately or following investigation.

Anyone can handle complaints. Perhaps the prime reason complainers demand to speak to the managing director or 'the manager' is because their complaints have been inadequately handled in the past. But those who will deal with complaints — and that could well be anyone in the section (why do the worst complaints always come in at lunchtime or when the office is half staffed?) — must be properly briefed. It is one of the processes in business where a strict progress of action is necessary.

*Dealing with complaints*

The following technique should deal with the majority of complaints. On the telephone or in person we should always act as follows:

1    *Listen* to all the facts, reassure the complainant frequently with 'Yes, I understand', and let him run out of steam. This gives us time to think about what we will say, and what action to take. Write down the details and get his name, telephone number etc. clearly, early on.
2    *Sympathise* and make him feel that we would feel the same way if we were in his shoes. Show him there will be no argument. Never interrupt with 'But'. Apologise, at least for his state of mind, and without necessarily taking the blame.
3    *Clarify* and make sure we have *all the facts* right. We should still keep away from arguing — the truth about the complaint may not be as it seems at first. Avoid 'doubt' phrases such as 'you claim' or 'as I understand it', which make the customer feel he is being disbelieved; that will only make him reinforce his complaint.
4    *Summarise* his complaint, which will serve to check that we have all the facts, and reassure the customer that we understand his problem — it will get him 'nodding' with us for the first time.

If at this point we have to check or investigate, it may be necessary to call back; certainly we should avoid keeping him holding on for long. We need to explain exactly what will now happen and how long it will take (a promise we *must* then keep — 'I will be back to you within an hour'). It will help the situation if we use our name and if possible assure him we will call him back personally. Anything less may sound evasive.

5    *Answering a justified complaint.* If possible, accept the blame and apologise unreservedly. Remember that the customer sees us in the sales office as sales person, production manager and invoice clerk; we personify for that moment the company. State what action we will take to put things right, even if our own action is merely to pass the complaint on (never downwards, however).

It is useful to give some perceived concession if possible, but not too much. We should try to do more than the minimum needed to put things right. Thank the customer ('for bringing this to our attention') and follow it up.

6 *Answering an unjustified complaint.* If the customer is mistaken or has got the wrong end of the stick, be diplomatic. If it is a misunderstanding, we can blame ourselves for not being clearer, and the instruction book, a letter, the invoice, etc. for being confusing. Try to allow him to correct himself and 'save face', e.g. 'Do you have the delivery note in front of you?' He may see his error before we have to point it out.

7 *Complaint follow-up.* We must always do whatever we promised to do for the customer and we must advise whoever else needs to know about the complaint (via the complaint form). But there is something else to remember.

A complaint is a contact with a customer, often a very close one, and one initiated by the customer. It can often be developed from a complaining call to a contented, ordering call — if not immediately, then soon. The easiest way to achieve this is to follow the technique above, and then do something extra.

Make a follow-up note in the diary or record card to ensure that we (personally):
(a) follow up to see if his complaint has been dealt with, if it concerned another division;
(b) contact the customer to enquire if he feels the complaint was brought to satisfaction;
(c) refer to the (satisfactory) outcome at the next contact;
(d) verify his next order by writing a letter and making him feel that we have taken notice of him, that we really do regret customers having to complain.

The same 'turn round' principles apply if we have to write a letter in answer to a complaint, though we should perhaps first ask ourselves if this is a sufficiently prompt way of handling the situation. The example in Figure 9.3 shows the negative upsetting approach, which can be replaced by something (Figure 9.4) that finds a way of letting the (mistaken) customer down lightly, still apologises and offers something seemingly extra. It is clear which approach is more likely to retain the customer's goodwill.

*Sales letters*

The volume of paper produced by business today is incalculable — memos in triplicate, invoices in quadruplicate, letters, confirmations, orders, reports, tenders, complaints ... and forms, forms and forms. There are also sales letters, leaflets, brochures.

No wonder that individual letters become diluted by the sea of paper around them and command little attention. The major consideration has become to move paperwork on as fast as possible before the next lot arrives: to file it — or preferably destroy it — quickly.

So it is well worth while considering how to get the best attention for what we write. We have already looked at writing letters in general, as part of the company image. Now we should remember the selling sequence and the buying process, and the stages we should try to move a customer through towards an order. It is clear then that:

## ALL LETTERS FROM THE SALES OFFICE TO THE CUSTOMER ARE SALES LETTERS IN OUR TERMS

These letters include the following:

1 Letters accompanying quotations.
2 Letters accompanying sales literature.
3 Letters answering or following up complaints.
4 Letters confirming appointments.
5 Letters giving our office or branch location etc.

**Marketing Improvements Limited**

Ulster House,
17 Ulster Terrace
Outer Circle Regents Park
London NW1 4PJ

Telephone 01-487 5811

Telex 299723 MARIMP G
Cables IMPMARK London NW1

European Office, 49 Avenue de l'Armee
1040 Brussels Telephone 733.47.39
Telex 63577 MI EUR B

---

PF/bw


21 January 1980.


N Smith Esq
Fortescues Foods Ltd
Fambridge Road
Newtown


Dear Mr Smith

Thank you for your letter of 20 January, 1980.   You
will see that you missed attending the seminar 'How
To Handle Major Customers Profitably' which you were
registered on for 18 January, 1980, because you
misread the joining instructions.   The enclosed copy
shows quite clearly that the correct details were
sent to you

If you want to try again, the programme repeats on
26 February, 1980, at the same venue.   You will need
to record your intention to attend in writing.

Yours sincerely,




PATRICK FORSYTH
Client Services Director
_____


Enclosure:

---

Directors: M.T.Wilson BA Minst.M.D. F.Wilson J.B.J.Lidstone Minst.MMBIM P.B.Kirkby MA. D.I.Senton.
Registered Office Ulster House, 17 Ulster Terrace Regents Park Outer Circle London NW1 4PJ.    Registration No 800303 England.
Licensed annually by the Westminster City Council for Executive Selection.

**Fig. 9.3 Poor complaint-handling letter**

**Marketing Improvements Limited**

Ulster House,
17 Ulster Terrace
Outer Circle Regents Park
London NW1 4PJ

Telephone 01-487 5811

Telex 299723 MARIMP G
Cables IMPMARK London NW1

European Office, 49 Avenue de l'Armee
1040 Brussels Telephone 733.47.39
Telex 63577 MI EUR B

---

PF/bw

21 January 1980


N Smith Esq
Fortescues Foods Ltd
Fambridge Road
Newtown



Dear Mr Smith

I was very sorry to hear, from your letter of 20 January,
1980, that you missed attending the seminar 'How To
Handle Major Customers Profitably' which you were
registered to attend on 18 January.

In view of the short notice on which you planned to
attend, whilst joining instructions sent to you did
give the correct date information, we perhaps should have
made it clearer.  My apologies.

Luckily the programme is scheduled to repeat again before
too long.  I have therefore moved your registration
forward to the next date ~ 26 February, 1980, at the
same venue ~ and hope you will be able to put this in
your diary now, whilst places remain free.  Information
about this and other future dates is enclosed.

Do let me know if this should not be convenient.
Meantime, I am sure you were able to put the unexpected
time at your disposal on 18 January to good use and that
you  will find the seminar useful when you attend on
26 February.  We look forward to meeting you.

Yours sincerely,



PATRICK FORSYTH
Client Services Director
─────────────────────────


Enclosure:

---

Directors: M.T.Wilson BA Minst.M.D. F.Wilson J.B.J.Lidstone Minst.MMBIM P.B.Kirkby MA. D.I.Senton.
Registered Office Ulster House, 17 Ulster Terrace Regents Park Outer Circle London NW1 4PJ.    Registration No 800303 England.
Licensed annually by the Westminster City Council for Executive Selection.

**Fig. 9.4  Good complaint-handling letter**

No matter what the subject of the letter is, we want to be sure that our letters will (a) command attention, (b) be understood, and (c) be acted upon (it is this that differentiates sales or persuasive communication from simple factual communication). If they are to do this, we have to take some care in preparing them; in this age of dictating machines and rush and pressure, it is too easy to just 'dash them off'.

*Preparing persuasive sales letters*

Before we even draft a letter we should remember the principles of selling, and in particular remember to see things through the customer's eyes. Then we should ask ourselves five questions:

1    For whom is the letter and its message intended? (This is not always the person it is addressed to).
2    What are their particular needs?
3    How does our product, service or proposition satisfy those needs — what benefits does it give?
4    What do we want the customer *to do* when he receives the letter? We must have a clear objective for every letter, and these objectives must be (a) commercially worth while, within the company strategy, (b) stated in terms of customer needs, (c) realistic and achievable with available resources, (d) specific, clear and time bounded, and (e) capable of evaluation with a Yes/No answer.
5    How does the customer take this action?

The last two questions are frequently forgotten, but they are very important. It should be perfectly clear in our own minds what we want the recipient to do, and very often this can be put equally clearly to the customer; but having achieved this, we can lose the advantage if lack of information makes it difficult for the customer to take the action we want him to. For example, we may fail to give him ordering details or a branch office's address, not tell him how to qualify for a special discount, and so on.

The principal object of writing a sales letter is to draw the reader's attention to the reasons why he should buy; and explaining what benefits he will gain is of paramount importance. It is therefore essential that we know for whom the letter and its message are intended. Most sales letters are addressed to three different types of customer and potential customer:

1    The retailer who needs to resell the produce.
2    The end-consumer, who has a need for it, for his own use.
3    The middleman, who needs it as part of something he provides for others.

The customer's reasons for buying the benefits he will gain must be related to the type of customer he is and what the product does for him, rather than what the product is. Description of the product and what its features are is one of the functions of the leaflets, catalogues or brochures which often accompany the letter.

Look again at Figure 7.3, which shows how to identify customer needs and how to relate the product features to the benefits the customer will receive. Familiarity with this process will make it easier to build up a databank of information which can be used selectively in sales letters — a choice of phrases and sentences can then easily be brought to mind for 'instant use' in letters to a variety of customer types.

*Criteria for successful sales letters*

Perhaps before anything else, a sales letter must be attractively laid out, grammatically correct and well typed. That will at least give the impression it has originated in an efficient and reputable company. The more prestigious and expensive the product, the more important this is. The rather untidy duplicated letter that is passable for products costing only a few pounds will not be acceptable for cameras, machine tools or engineering contracts. A company selling a service should try particularly to convey neatness and efficiency as a cornerstone of the image, and it would be let down by sloppy sales letters.

The letter should be personalised if possible. Again, when the product or service is expensive or 'up market', one assumes that the company will take the trouble to get the customer's own name. It does give the impression that we have a message which will be of particular interest to him, and it shows that we take enough trouble to find out exactly who our customers are. Do not ruin it, however, by wrong spelling, wrong initials or using a job title that he was promoted from 4 years ago. On other occasions, when for quantity reasons personalised greetings are not possible, there are an endless number of opening words to worry over:

| | |
|---|---|
| Dear Sir | Dear Car Owner |
| Dear Madam | Dear Gardener |
| Dear Sir/Madam | Dear Holiday-maker |
| Dear Householder | Dear Customer |
| Dear Reader | ... even Hello, Hi! or Greetings! |

None of these are anything more than token greetings, and can have little impact on the recipient, though perhaps almost anything is better than 'Dear Sir'.

Reproduction letters should be avoided where possible. There are very few good ways of doing bulk reproduction without them appearing to be just that. Any good that has been achieved by a personal solution can be lost immediately if the person's name is an obvious addition to a standard letter churned off a stencil duplicator. Computer-addressed letters are only marginally better, for most users still employ a pre-printed letter, and however good the printing, the additions are seldom well-aligned, and again the effect is lost. A good sales letter for an expensive product deserves to be fully addressed and typed by the same machine, and this can be done automatically.

The role of 'form' letters is a separate issue. Let us look specifically at the individual letter, though similar factors apply to the content of both.

The most important part of a letter is the first sentence. It will determine whether the rest of the letter is read. People seldom read a letter in the same sequence in which it was written. Their eyes flick from the sender's address to the ending, then to the greeting and the first sentence, skim to the last — and then, if the sender is lucky, back to the first sentence for a more careful reading of the whole letter. Research has been done showing a clear sequence (see Figure 9.5), so the first sentence is about the only chance we have of 'holding' the reader, and it should arouse immediate interest.

But gimmicks should be avoided. They invariably give the reader the impression of being talked down to. So how can we achieve the best opening?

*The opening*

Write out the name of the person you are writing to. Seeing it written down will help you visualise his point of view. When possible, always address the letter to a person rather than to 'Dear Sir'. It is much less formal, everyone likes hearing his own name, and unless we write 'personal' on the envelope there is no fear that the letter will lie unanswered in his absence.

Keep references short and subject headings to the point — his point. Do not use 'Re'.

Make sure the start of the letter will (a) command attention, (b) gain interest, and (c) lead easily into the main text. For example:

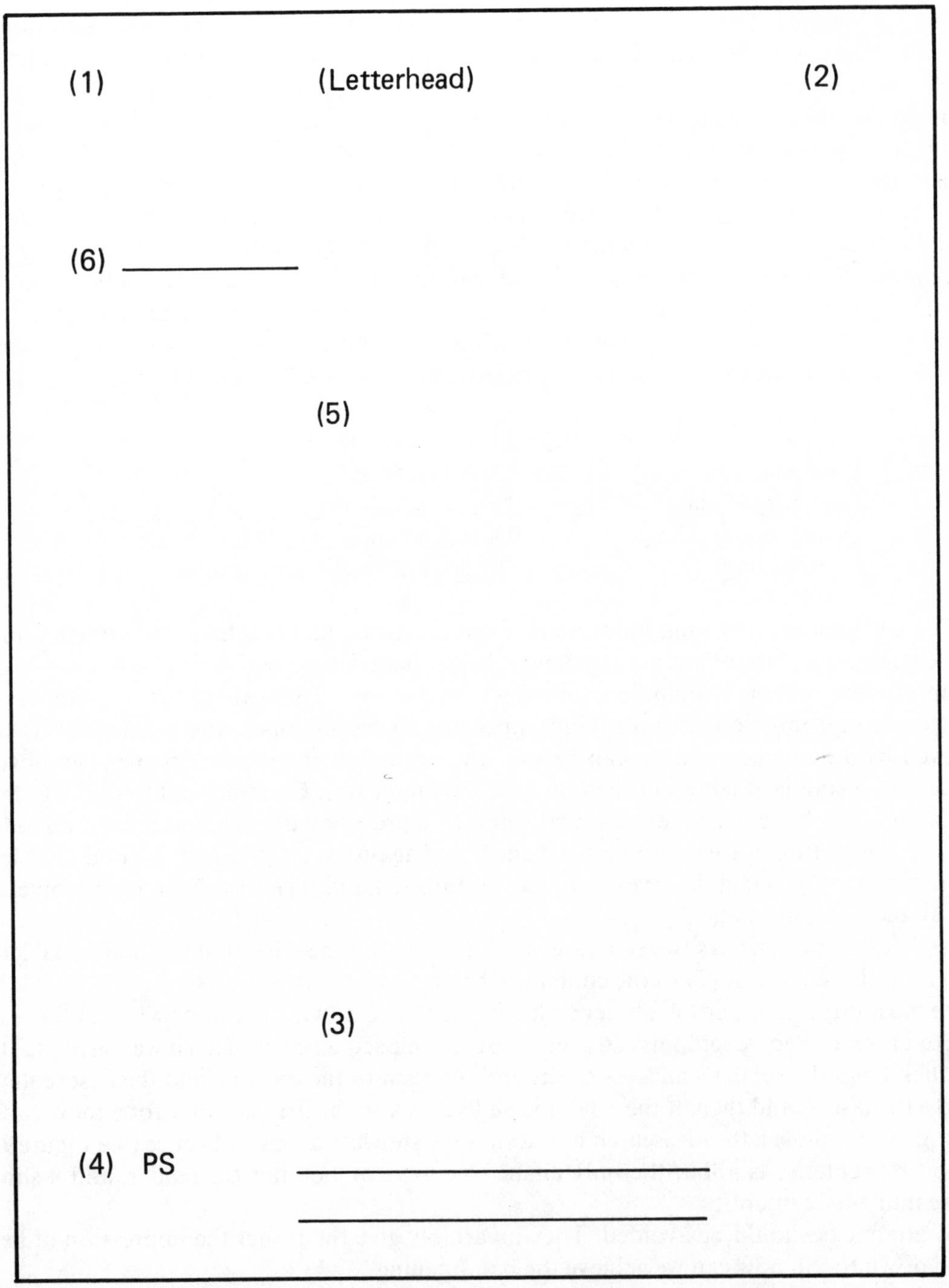

```
┌─────────────────────────────────────────────────┐
│                                                   │
│  (1)              (Letterhead)              (2)   │
│                                                   │
│                                                   │
│  (6) ──────────                                   │
│                                                   │
│                                                   │
│                      (5)                          │
│                                                   │
│                                                   │
│                                                   │
│                                                   │
│                                                   │
│                                                   │
│                                                   │
│                                                   │
│                                                   │
│                      (3)                          │
│                                                   │
│                                                   │
│  (4)  PS         ─────────────────────────        │
│                  ─────────────────────────        │
│                                                   │
└─────────────────────────────────────────────────┘
```

(1), (2), (3) — information, taken in very fast. Who is it from?

(4) — if there is one, the PS is the 'most read part of any letter'.

(5) — an overall scan — do I have to read it all? — use of headings will affect this view.

(6) — from beginning on (provided the opening is effective).

**Fig. 9.5 Sales letters: reading sequence**

1   Ask a 'Yes' question.
2   Tell him why you are writing to him particularly.
3   Tell him why he should read the letter.
4   Flatter him (carefully).
5   Tell him what he might lose if he ignores the message.
6   Give him some 'mind bending' news (if you have any).

## *The body of the letter*

The body of the letter runs straight on from the opening. It must consider the reader's needs or problems from his point of view. It must interest him. It must get the reader nodding in agreement — 'Yes, I wish you could help me on that'.

Of course we are able to help him. In drafting we write down what we intend for him and of course list the benefits, not features, and in particular benefits which will help him solve that problem and satisfy that need.

We have to anticipate his possible objections to our proposition in order to select our strongest benefits and most convincing answers. If there is a need to counter objections, then we may need to make our letter longer and give proof, e.g. comment from a third party, that our benefits are genuine. However, remember to keep the letter as short as possible.

It is easy to find ourselves quoting the sales literature to the customer. If we were writing a lecture on the subject, we would probably need all that information. When writing to a customer, we have to select just one or two benefits which will be of particular use to him in his situation, and which support the literature.

Our aims are the following:

1   To keep the reader's immediate interest.
2   Keep that interest with the best benefit.
3   Win him over with a second benefit.
4   Obtain action by a firm close.

## *The letter ending*

In drafting we can make a (short) summary of the benefits to him of our proposition. Having decided on what action we are wanting the reader to take, we must be positive about getting it.

It is necessary to nudge the reader into action with a decisive close. Do not use

'We look forward to hearing',
'I trust you have given ...',
'... favour of your instructions',
'... doing business with you',
'I hope I can be of further assistance',

which are phrases added as padding between the last point and 'Yours sincerely', but the following:

1   *The alternative close*
    (a)   ask him to telephone or write;
    (b)   telephone collect or use the reply paid envelope;
    (c)   send bankers' references or cash with order.
2   *Concession close*
    (a)   we shall be able to let you have the current prices if you order now;
    (b)   our normal delivery is 2 months, but since you are one of our best ...

3    *Direct request*
   (a)  please clear the outstanding payment so we can continue shipments;
   (b) please post your order today so we can deliver this week.

In signing off do not automatically use 'Yours faithfully' for 'Dear Sir', and 'Yours sincerely' when the letter is addressed to an individual, but match to the tone of your general approach. Make sure your name is typed, and if it will help the reader, add your position. Sign the letter yourself whenever possible, and consider letting your secretary use her own name rather than 'pp' if you are not able to sign.

If you use a postscript make sure it is a final benefit — an extra help to closing. Remember a PS gets read, so do not regard it as just for omissions but consider how you can use it. ,

Finally let us consider the language we use in such letters. Many people have acquired the habit of artificiality in writing, approaching it quite differently from their way of talking to a customer, and in a way that lessens the danger of making a sale.

*The language*

Remember our intention is to prompt the customer to action rather than demonstrate our 'Oxford English'. We should write much as we speak.

The following are some useful rules:

| | |
|---|---|
| *Be clear* | — Make sure the message is straightforward and uncluttered by 'padding'. Use short words and phrases. Avoid jargon. |
| *Be natural* | — Do not behave or project yourself differently just because it is in writing. |
| *Be positive* | — In tone and emphasis (be helpful). |
| *Be courteous* | — Always. |
| *Be efficient* | — Project the right image. |
| *Be personal* | — Use 'I' — say what *you* will do. |
| *Be appreciative* | — Thank you is a good phrase |

Figure 9.6 will help us examine specific aspects of the language we use in letters.

---

*Avoid trite openings*
We respectfully acknowledge receipt of...
I have to acknowledge with thanks...
Yours of even date to hand...
We have pleasure in attaching...
Referring to your communication of...
The contents of which are noted...
This letter is for the purpose of requesting...
If we follow the rules for a good opening, we shall also rarely begin with 'Thank you for your letter of...'

*Avoid pomposity*                                                                                              *List alternative*
We beg to advise...
The position with regard to...
It will be appreciated that...
It is suggested that the reason...
The undersigned/writer...
May we take this opportunity of...

Fig. 9.6 Sales letters: use of language

Allow me to say in this instance...
Which you claim/state...
For your information...
Having regard to the fact that...
We should point out that...
Answering in the affirmative/negative...
We are giving the matter every consideration
We are not in a position to...
The opportunity is taken to mention...
Despatched under separate cover...

*Avoid coldness and bad psychology*                                    *List alternative*
Advise/inform
Desire
Learn/note
Obtain
Regret
Trust
Your complaint/dissatisfaction
Dictated but not read by...

*Avoid cliché endings*
Thanking you in advance...
Assuring you of our best attention at all times, we remain...
Regretting our inability to be of service in this matter...
Trusting we may be favoured with...
Awaiting a favourable reply...
Please do not hesitate to...

*Do keep it simple — prefer short words to the following long ones*
Additional
Alteration
Anticipate
Appreciable
Approximately
Assistance
Beneficial
Considerable
                                                                       *List alternative*
Consequently
Commencement
Co-operation
Deficiencies
Despatch
Discontinue
Discussion
Duplicate
Elucidate
Emphasis
Encounter
Endeavour
Envisage

**Fig. 9.6 (cont.)**

Facilitate
Finalise
Fundamental
Generate
However
Immediately
Implementation
Initiate
Locality
Manufacture
Materialise
Merchandise
Necessitates
Nevertheless
Numerous
Objective
Obtain

*List alternative*

Optimum
Practically
Purchase (verb)
Problematical
Requirements
Sufficient
Termination
Utilise
*Prefer one or two words to several*
According to our records...
A large majority of...
A percentage of...
Along the lines of...
At a later date...
At this precise moment in time...
Due to the fact that...
Facilities are provided for...
Generally speaking in this connection...
I am inclined to the view that...
In the event that the foregoing...
In the initial stages...
In the neighbourhood of...
In the not too distant future...
It is not possible to effect delivery...
On the occasion of...
Prior to this, we experienced trouble with...
There can be no doubt about...

*List alternative*

The position will soon be reached that...
Should the situation arise that we are unable...
We are prepared to admit...
We shall not be in a position to...

Fig. 9.6 (cont.)

With a view to/in order to...
With regard to...
With the result that...

**Fig. 9.6 (cont.)**

---

*Telephone techniques*

The telephone is a powerful means of communication and is far more suitable for moving many contacts into a further stage of the selling sequence than the sales letter. But its obvious advantages are often not made use of, and its limitations are sometimes not appreciated either.

The main benefits of the telephone are the following:

1   *Cost.* It is far cheaper than a representative calling in person, and frequently more economic than writing. Remember the comparison with a letter is not only between the cost of a telephone call and the stamps — we must add stationery, dictation time, typing, checking etc. as well.

2   *Speed.* Questions, alternative choices etc. can often be dealt with immediately and decisions reached in minutes, whereas doing it all by correspondence would take days or weeks. However, if the contact starts with a customer's letter, a written reply may well be expected; though an immediate phone call on an urgent matter may be appreciated, and written confirmation can follow. The speed of immediate response during the conversation also means we must be 'quicker on our feet'.

3   *Accuracy.* There are many benefits in communicating when both parties have access to the back-up information they keep on their desks and in their offices; a buyer or representative can be limited to what he carries in his briefcase. Doubtful points can be clarified immediately, though important figures, dates, specifications, etc. should always be confirmed in writing as soon as possible.

4   *Quantity.* All the above benefits mean that sales office staff, in many cases, do as much selling from their desks as the outside representatives — often even more. What they cannot do because they are not on the spot can be made up for by being able to contact many more customers in a day.

Thus, as well as response to telephone enquiries, written enquiries can be handled by phone (and of course in writing), especially if the enquiry or complaint is urgent or serious. (In addition, as we will see in the next chapter, the sales office can itself initiate contact.)

But the telephone also has a number of limitations, and the problems which 'voice only' communication pose are considerable; we only have to try describing some everyday object, without using gestures or illustrations, to appreciate this. Describing something unfamiliar or a colour or a pattern is even more difficult.

Because of these limitations, telephone calls should be planned. We must even plan how incoming enquiries are to be handled. Planning is essential for the following reasons:

1   To overcome tension or nervousness.
2   To assist our ability to think fast enough.
3   To set clear and specific objectives designed to gain agreement and a specific commitment from the customer.
4   To prevent side-tracking (or being side-tracked, if we keep coming back to our plan).
5   To enable us to talk from the listener's point of view.
6   To enable us to measure our own effectiveness.

*Planning telephone response*

The worst things about telephones is that they are intrusive and can take us by surprise. No matter what we are doing, someone else can interrupt us, and without warning plunge us into handling a complaint, trying to counter claims about competitive products, coping with a difficult order, making awkward delivery commitments, and so on. We should always have a plan to give us the maximum opportunity to deal promptly with each situation.

This does not mean we adopt a 'scripted' or parrot-like approach, but that we intend, and plan, to control the direction of the conversation towards a specific objective. It helps to think of this graphically (see Figure 9.7) — rather as the captain of a ship, proceeding across an open sea and subject to the impact of wind and weather, might take a number of courses, though the clear position of his destination will allow him to correct and keep on track.

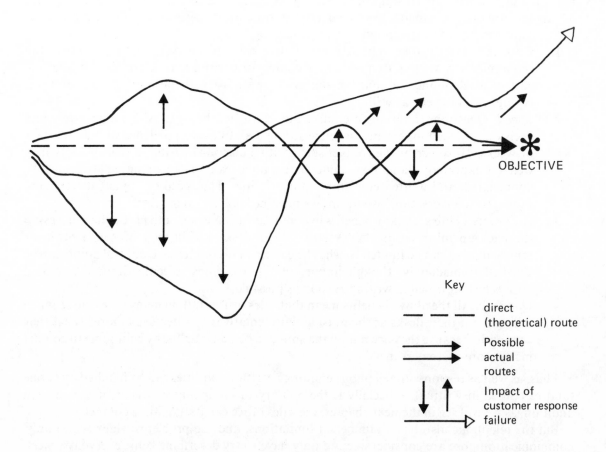

OBJECTIVE

Key

– – – – direct (theoretical) route

→ Possible actual routes

↓↑ Impact of customer response

——▷ failure

**Fig. 9.7 Structuring and directing the telephone call towards our objective**

We must keep in mind the classic stages of the sale. Remember what we said about the switchboard operator earlier in the book — the opening of a telephone call, like a face-to-face call, must create the best possible impression with the customer. Start with a courteous 'Good morning' or 'Good afternoon' rather than a bald 'Yes' or 'Hallo', and then identify yourself by name and job title.

The first few words can often be lost at the start of a telephone conversation, so that, to ensure that we get our name over, it may be worth repeating: thus '... this is Smith, XYZ Ltd, John Smith...' This sounds natural, ensures the message gets across and allows a job title or departmental description to be added if we wish.

If we are contacting the customer in response to a previous call or letter, we should always greet the customer by name, then identify ourselves and our company, clearly.

Naturally a call that we make to a customer can be planned far better than an incoming call, when all our initial actions are purely responsive. Incoming calls, though some will be totally unpredictable, usually form a pattern. So, for example, we can plan the best way to handle calls resulting from a current advertising campaign. We should follow a planned sequence in either case, and everything we have discovered so far on handling objections or on writing letters should be borne in mind.

Clarity is perhaps the most important factor. We must be clear exactly who we are speaking to, what position and responsibility he has, and, above all, what the subject of the call is.

In the sales office the majority of calls will come from, and be to, customers and potential customers. The next stage in the plan is therefore to find out what the listener wants — he will not always be lucidly forthcoming himself on this — and write it down. It is a golden rule never to deal on the telephone without a pen and paper (or enquiry form). The two most effective ways of doing this are the following:

1   *Questioning Method* — asking open questions to identify our customer's specific needs or problems. For example:

'Is this for exterior or interior use?'
'What loads will the unit have to bear?'
'Will you need to use many accessories?'

The questions will depend on the products we sell.

Alternatively our questions can be tailored to gain background information to enable us to suit our presentation to the customer's requirements:

'You have previously used our TX30 model, haven't you?'
'I suppose you are still heavily involved in the Latin American market?'
'Will this be for your new plant in Cumbria?'

2   *Statement method.* Where sufficient information is already known a statement of the unique quality of our product or service, and how that will especially help him, can be an effective start. A statement of how the product or service can satisfy a need or a problem which has previously been identified can also be successful.

'As you've been increasingly involved in off-shore oil, you will be interested to know that we are opening a service depot in Aberdeen next month...'
'The new coating will completely prevent the fading problems you have always experienced with exterior applications..'

By adopting this approach to our telephone calls, we show the customer our concern for helping him, and for not just selling our company's products and services. He will appreciate the fact. We will seem to be a company which is more likely to satisfy his needs.

Whether we ask questions or make statements, we should soon arouse some interest in our product or service, and then we should briefly summarise the customer's needs: 'So your prime requirements are early delivery, and guaranteed service and replacement costs...' This will show him that we have understood his situation, and it clarifies in our own minds the major facts. It also ideally sets the scene for the next stage.

From the information we have gained about his needs, we select the benefits and features of our product or service which will satisfy him. (If necessary, our summarising of his needs can be 'adjusted' so that we select those benefits where we score highest over competitors.). Now we can:

1   Sell those benefits and features.
2   Sell any other advantages (price, service discount, etc.).

3   Get the customer to agree that these are genuine advantages.

4   Gain the customer's agreement that our product or service could be an advantage.

Not every call runs like clockwork and not every customer is totally satisfied with what we offer or say. We must plan for these situations too.

Ideally we should try to anticipate likely objections before making/taking the call. If we do, then we can build these into the presentation alongside genuine compensatory remarks. If he raises unforeseen objections:

1   Let the customer talk, don't interrupt (jumping in too quickly can sound glib).

2   Be sympathetic ('Yes, I can see that would inconvenience you.').

3   Don't argue — *ever*.

4   Summarise the objection before answering.

5   Let the customer down gently if he has not understood your proposition and expects something he cannot have.

6   Be constructive when answering — never imply that you don't care if you don't get his order.

7   Surround the objection or bad points with other benefits ('Delivery *is* longer, but you will have the advantage of the improved design, and the price is no different — and it includes delivery.').

Do not worry if you cannot overcome some objections; not all will weigh against the balance sufficiently for the customer to say 'no'. For most purchases a buying decision occurs not when all objections are overcome but when the positive elements outweigh the possible snags. Our job is not to remove all objections but to get the balance right.

Obtaining the commitment is the ultimate objective of all selling. If the customer does not place an order, now or in the future, we will have failed in our objective. Not every call can result in an order, of course, for some sales take a while to complete; but each call should take the prospect to some specific further stage in the buying process or it will not have succeeded.

From the customer's point of view, his needs have to be identified, discussed, and a desire for the product or service created before any action is willingly taken or a commitment given. Most people hesitate to make decisions, and if the consequences of a wrong decision are likely to be severe, then we hesitate even more. The customer is quite likely to be reluctant to make a firm decision, being unsure that the proposition will work. He may often even seek our reassurance and help that he is making the right decision. We should avoid silences when the call enters this closing stage, and rather repeat benefits, or help him to make a decision by asking closing questions, such as 'Will you want this charged, or will you send a cheque and benefit from the extra discount?'

When we have secured the order or commitment, we should wind up as follows:

1   Thank the customer.

2   Confirm what follow-up action we propose or is necessary (if any).

3   Make sure that each party has all necessary information, such as full names and addresses, delivery address, order numbers, quantities, etc.

4   Sometimes build up goodwill further by briefly mentioning benefits once more.

5   Ring off, 'fast but last'. Many a sale has been lost by the salesman chatting on, only to find the customer checking back and deciding '... on thinking about that a bit more I am not sure...'

*Telephone sales hints*

1   Plan the call, if possible. Research the customer before the call, and keep his file at hand. Ensure files are accessible for inward calls.

2   Always have catalogues, price lists, delivery schedules close by, and perhaps in special form, e.g. 'drum' style card indexes or on wall charts.
3   Explore the customer's needs, with open questions.
4   Always make notes during the call.
5   Offer alternatives if what he asks for is unavailable, and mention benefits to offset his disappointment: 'I'm sorry but the 12-inch model will not be in for at least three months, but the 18-inch is practically as light, just as cheap to run, and of course does far more than the smaller model.
6   Do not just baldly state the price, but give other information he will be pleased to hear: 'The more powerful 12-inch model is only about £20 extra, and apart from the better cutting capabilities it has a newly improved frame, making it much more rigid.'
7   Always see the product or service through the customer's eyes, bear in mind his needs, and stress benefits.
8   Listen to objections without arguing, but meet them with benefits — e.g. with price, and offer value answers.
9   Repeat important details to be certain.
10  Be ready to suggest other sales possibilities, perhaps to the same contact, perhaps to another part of his company: 'I suppose you are the major user in your company, but do you know if any other department is likely to use...'

# 10: Initiated Activities

We should never lose sight of the principal objective of the whole sales organisation, which is to sell the company's products or services. It exists to win orders.

The sales office is an integral part of the sales organisation — not an administrative wing, but a vital part of the selling operation. This is so easily forgotten, but a sales office which becomes principally concerned with 'firefighting', with sorting out problems, and which regards itself as the 'paperwork section' of sales, runs the following risks:

1    Of hiding weakness in the other parts of the organisation. Whether in sales, warehouse and delivery, invoicing etc.
2    Of becoming over-staffed and over-expensive.
3    Of rescuing rather than contributing to sales turnover.
4    Of failing to recognise priorities.

The effective sales office, however, is uniquely placed to initiate a number of actions, and stimulating new or additional business should be one of its prime considerations. With the right approach, it will soon become a habit for members of the sales office to become 'sales minded', so that opportunities are grasped whenever they present themselves. Opportunities for new and additional business can arise from the following sources:

1    Enquiries from prospective customers.
2    Comments contained in customer correspondence.
3    Orders, which can create a repeat demand immediately, or in the future.
4    Comments on representatives' reports.
5    Complaints.
6    Hearing about new applications of existing products.
7    News of competitive activity.

All these are sources of information which, if followed through, could easily lead to new customers and to further business with existing customers.

Spotting the information in these cases is a creative process which is partly a habit — that is, it becomes easier and more natural to do the more frequently it is done.

*Enquiries* are a natural originator of sales. Rather than simply respond to the enquiry and leave the next step to the enquirer, we should lead the customer into the next stage of the buying process by asking questions, making leading statements etc., as we have already discussed. Often we may be able to lead the enquirer right through to placing an order.

*Correspondence* with customers could provide openings for new sales. A request for an accessory could lead to the sale of a new improved model. A change of address could mean larger premises, expansion and more sales. Reading 'between the lines' can be an interesting and profitable habit to get into.

*Orders* should never be thought of as the end of a cycle of events but the beginning of the next. Very few individuals and even fewer firms only buy one of something throughout their lives. When a customer orders *one*, we should make certain that he does not need *two*, or try to establish when the next may be needed.

If that is not too far in the future, we can work towards ensuring that we get the order next time as well. No matter how far in the future, we should at least try to ensure customer satisfaction, so that when he is next in need, he will return to us, and not a competitor. The same applies of course to other products in the range. If he wants A can he be persuaded to take B from us as well?

*Representatives' reports* and the comments they make can suggest approaches which lead to making further sales, both with particular representatives and customers, and with others. They may identify a particular way to do a sales demonstration, a certain line of reasoning, an installation technique, an application not previously envisaged.

Do not forget to feedback to representatives any useful information obtained in this way. Most salesmen hate, and therefore sometimes skimp, filling in reports. If we can demonstrate the value of their comments, they will be more inclined to make them and the whole process gains.

*Complaints*, as we have already seen, can frequently be turned into new sales, provided they are handled correctly. Not only can the complainer become a re-orderer, but if complaints indicate a fault in the system or product, we can put it right before other complaints come in — and gain some prestige for awareness. If a modification results, that opens new sales opportunities, too.

*New applications* always result in new sales, for it is like discovering a whole new market no one knew existed. News of new applications can be got from customers direct, from representatives' reports, and from trade and technical magazines. The best thing about new applications is that even if they are first discovered with a competitor's products, we can still benefit from the 'new market'. Sometimes this process gives rise to major new market areas, e.g. the use of scaffolding, outside the construction industry, for temporary seating at, for instance, sports events.

### Kinds of initiated activity

There are two kinds:

1  Activity solely within the sales office area of responsibility.
2  Activity demanding liaison with the sales force, or with others.

Exactly what falls within each of these will vary between companies, and needs defining and agreeing, so that 'no wires are crossed'. In some companies a wide degree of autonomy may be given to the sales office; in others the sales office may only be able to handle certain types of queries on its own, or certain categories of customers; and in the third category the sales office may have to refer at all stages to the sales force or the sales manager, or may not be able to initiate stock activity without the purchasing division's permission.

There should always be as much delegation as possible to ensure effective management, and

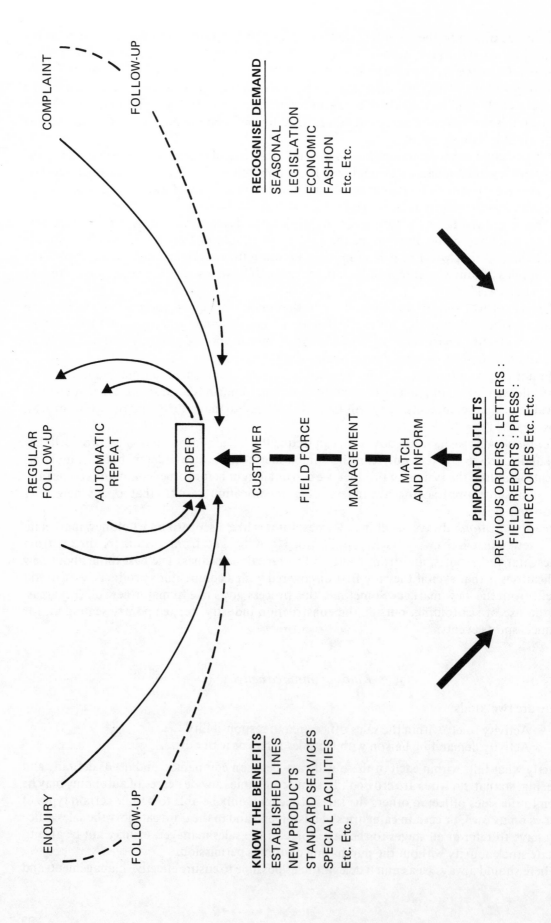

Fig. 10.1 Generating ongoing turnover from the sales office

COMPLAINT

FOLLOW-UP

RECOGNISE DEMAND
SEASONAL
LEGISLATION
ECONOMIC
FASHION
Etc. Etc.

REGULAR
FOLLOW-UP

AUTOMATIC
REPEAT

ORDER

CUSTOMER

FIELD FORCE

MANAGEMENT

MATCH
AND INFORM

PINPOINT OUTLETS
PREVIOUS ORDERS : LETTERS :
FIELD REPORTS : PRESS :
DIRECTORIES Etc. Etc.

KNOW THE BENEFITS
ESTABLISHED LINES
NEW PRODUCTS
STANDARD SERVICES
SPECIAL FACILITIES
Etc. Etc.

ENQUIRY

FOLLOW-UP

there is nothing to gain by keeping a sales office composed purely of responsive 'functionaries'. The sales operation is a creative and exciting part of business, and keeping people within that operation, yet forbidding them to take part in the more satisfying aspects of it, leads to a dispirited staff which cannot give of its best.

In any sales office it should be possible to set up a system which will regularly enable the sales office to act as follows:

1    Handle certain small accounts and/or small orders exclusively (notifying the rest of the sales operation if necessary). Indeed, economic factors may dictate this.
2    Chase stock replacement orders, and save customers/distributors going out of stock.
3    Introduce new lines (even if only to the point of the initial or advance notification).
4    Inform all customers about price changes, sales promotions etc.

One key method adopted by increasing numbers of companies in a variety of industries is some form of planned outgoing 'telesales' activity. For certain kinds of business and situations this can have considerable impact on sales and cost saving, or both. It is, however, something that has to be set up very carefully if it is to work effectively. For those who wish to consider this area in more detail; Appendix 1 (p.103) sets out in checklist form some of the aspects and criteria important to success.

Benefits from such systems can be twofold — sales can be increased directly, and valuable (and expensive) representative time can be freed for other tasks, particularly increasing time spent in face-to-face selling or negotiation. All of this can be handled by telephone or by letter (as in response activities), and it is only important to ensure that there is a proper feed of information into the record system, and a proper liaison with the sales force or its management, or any other division concerned.

These initiated activities, carried out constantly and regularly, can become an important function of the sales office, and a vital part of the whole sales operation. The actual generation of turnover by the sales office, as an interlocking cycle of events is illustrated by the diagram in Figure 10.1.

# 11:

# Support Activities

Unlike response activities and initiated activities, the sales office's support activities may have a less direct influence on sales. But that does not detract from their importance; the support function is a major activity for all sales offices, no matter how much or how little responsibility and opportunity they may have for response and initiated activities.

The support that an effective sales office can give to the sales field force is often vital to the success of the whole enterprise. Such support is so important that it must be sales-orientated even though it does not directly cause sales, and this is appreciated by the management in many successful companies. The value of good support is made clearer by an understanding of the function of the field force.

### Role of the field sales force

By the nature of their work, salesmen are often isolated, and only a small amount of their time is spent with the support of an office and an organisation physically about them. Equally, only a small amount of time is actually spent face to face with customers (often as little as 15 — 25 per cent of their working time). Yet unless they are busy selling, they cannot be seen to be 'earning their keep'.

A field sales force can be compared to a sophisticated modern aircraft, which is only undertaking its proper function when it is in flight, carrying passengers. How soon it can again be 'effective' depends on how quickly it can safely get back in the air after each flight, and that depends on the effectiveness of its ground support.

A salesman's success and effectiveness is dependent on only two major factors: (a) how often they are in the selling situation, and (b) what they do when they are.
Being in a 'selling situation' is not simply a matter of making calls — they must be the right calls. Effectiveness is therefore dependent on both *planning and selling*.

PLANNING — who to see
     — how many
     — how often

SELLING     — what is done

The sales office, as we shall see, can help in both planning and selling, by increasing representative selling time (e.g. by making appointments) and by influencing positively their ability to be effective face to face (e.g. by providing detailed and accurate information about customer needs).

The importance of the factors behind salesmen's success is usually highlighted by various costs and ratios established by sales management and regularly calculated by the sales office, as follows:

1   *Cost per call* — worked out for each representative, and a figure management is always keen to reduce owing to the high and rising total cost of keeping a salesman 'on the road'.

2   *Costs to order value* — comparison with an optimum figure, and comparison between all representatives will put paid to the frequent 'sales at any cost' habits encountered in some sales forces.

3   *Calls to order* — helps show the effectiveness of a salesman's technique.

There may be a number of other ratios and costs that are particularly important to one company, but in all cases it is variation from an established norm that is important, or comparison between different results. Frequently the sales office calculating these ratios and costs will only be required to submit them to sales management on an 'exception' basis — that is, when they exceed an agreed tolerance.

## Liaison between field force and sales office

This is obviously extremely important, and management should do everything it can to ensure that there is a two-way spirit of co-operation, for this is not something that occurs automatically in many companies. Too often there is friction. The sales office is not there just for support and donkey work, nor is it only there to breathe down the field force's neck and trumpet warnings when a salesman incurs too many expenses.

A good way to engender liaison and co-operation is to link sales office personnel with members of the field force, particularly as a service to customers. The salesman can then leave office contact names with clients, and sales office personnel may also be identified in sales literature, on business cards, or other literature.

This is particularly important for post-sales service, and for periods of negotiations when the salesmen are likely to be out of the office most of the time. Certain modern equipment — for example, a telephone or paging system in a salesman's car — can add to the impact of such liaison on the customer. In an area of activity where speed of response is essential it may be cost-effective and worth considering. Allocation of sales office/field force links can be by groups or categories of customers by products, by geographic areas etc., whichever is most appropriate.

More than anything else, however, the value of a sales office will be appreciated through the effectiveness of its support and degree of its input. Apart from general support and liaison, there are three key ways in which the sales office can have this essential input, and which aid salesmen's success by improving their planning and their selling. These are the regular provision of information, making appointments, and gaining information about particular situations.

## Provision of information

The sales force gets much of its information from the sales office. But there is a two-way information flow, for it has to pass back reports, orders, travelling expenses etc. Invariably certain information is regularly passed to the salesman, and how this is presented depends on the ingenuity of the management. Some companies use a weekly newsletter (or audio-tape) for information affecting all salesmen, and attractively presented sheets with individual information. Some information is presented in a way that allows updating in ring binders; but however information is presented, assorted sizes of paper with a variety of layouts and a general lack of consistency should be avoided. We want the information to be read, understood, kept, referred to and used for as long as necessary.

Regular information is likely to include the following:

1   Hints on new selling approaches.
2   Production news about new applications, warnings about complications or faults, news about developments and modifications etc.
3   The price: amendments to price list, with clear date application; changes to discounts; individual information on discounts to particular accounts; aids such as tables showing effect of high discounts and trade-ins; advice on credit restrictions etc. All these items are subject to regular and frequent change these days.
4   Advance notice about promotional activity: advertising campaigns, TV advertisements, advertisements in local press and on local radio, guest appearances, publicity campaigns, etc., and promotional material to back up campaigns, sales aids, displays etc.
5   Company organisational factors: news about staff appointments and changes, notification about meetings, training schedules, changes in procedures, changes of address, news of new branches, etc.
6   Competitive activity: news of new competitive products and new competitors, opening of new competitors' branches; information as for our own products, but concerning competitor products (the sales office often acts as a 'clearing house' for information about the competition, much of it coming from individual salesmen themselves).
7   Statistical information: sales figures, individual ratios, stock levels, discount average, relevant market trends, exchange rates, production figures and extimates, forecasts — any figures at all which can help the salesmen, directly or indirectly, to obtain an order.
8   Appointments with customers, individual information (discussed more fully below).
9   Enquiry information, also usually individual information (and again discussed more fully below).

### Making appointments

A salesman's productivity improves markedly if a number of his calls are by appointment. In some types of business or industry the majority of calls may have to be by appointment, and in any business there are always some companies which actively discourage or even forbid salesmen from 'dropping in' without an appointment.

Appointments may therefore be made for any of the usual call reasons: (a) in response to an enquiry, (b) as part of normal call frequency, (c) for a 'cold canvass', and (d) in special circumstances, e.g. after a complaint. In all these cases the sales office could quite easily make the appointment for the salesman, saving him time and perhaps providing a better service to the customer — always provided there has been some instruction and training and that we know when the salesmen are available.

Appointments will usually be made by phone, and before we even dial the customer's number, we must have at hand the following:

1   All customer information available to date, including the salesman's 'personal hints' card, which can help us avoid gaffes such as the wrong pronunciation of the customer's name.

2 Information on the availability of the salesman and similar information on the customer, e.g. the record card might state 'away at HQ on Friday', so we do not make a Friday appointment.

3 A checklist of what information we ideally want — other equipment being used by the customer, customer's preferences, size of company, etc.

The next step is to *get through to the right person*. The best way to do this is (a) to ask for who you want, confidently, (b) if asked, give your name and/or your company but no more, and (c) if you can speak to a secretary, offer a suitable alternative, e.g. 'Can you make an appointment, or would you prefer I spoke to Mr Smith?' You will not always succeed, but such a procedural approach will certainly help.

A structured approach with the buyer will have a greater chance of success than attempts at 'one-off' conversations. The following steps are advisable: 1 Check that you are through to the right person.

2 State your name and company (and repeat the company name, and the name of the representative concerned at least once).

3 Give your reason for calling.

4 Ask for any additional information that will be needed, or will be desirable at this stage.

5 Give reasons for the appointment (rather than some other means of proceeding) in terms of benefits to the customer. Speak of the meeting as 'working with the customer'.

6 Allow reasonable lead time, for the customer. He is less likely to refuse an appointment for 10 days' time than he is to refuse an appointment for tomorrow.

7 Offer an alternative — 'Would 3.00 p.m. Thursday afternoon be suitable, or would you prefer the morning, say Wednesday morning?' — with the first option more precisely stated than the second.

Now and again resistance will be met, but we can then employ an objection-handling technique. The 'boomerang' technique is particularly useful for 'turning' an objection. For instance:

> *Buyer*: 'It's not convenient — I haven't the time'.
> *Sales office*: 'It's because we know you're busy that we have prepared a special presentation, which will only take 10 minutes (be honest), and it will give you the opportunity to inspect the product well in advance of its general release ... we do expect demand to be very heavy.'

When we have got the buyer back on the track again, and sounding even tentatively agreeable, we can 'close' again as fast as is polite — just as if we were making a sales call, with the appointment as the objective.

If it is impossible to make an appointment, we can still save the situation to some degree by getting new information for the salesman's records, and making it qualify as a sales call. Having 'won' the conversation and 'negotiation' to that point, the buyer will often be in the frame of mind to allow us some concessions, and may be quite willing to give us information about competitive products, his uses of that product range, names of others in his organisation we could contact, etc.

Finally consider the impact of just when an appointment is timed. Such placing as first thing in the morning, last thing in the afternoon, or immediately after lunch, can help make the day far more productive. Additionally bear in mind that not everyone works the same day: one often hears representatives saying 'no one will see me before 10.00 a.m.' but for some customers 'first thing' means 8.15 a.m. and may provide a salesman with an uninterrupted hour (before the customer's switchboard opens) and a good start to his day.

*Gaining information*

It is impossible for salesmen to plan their calls properly without information about (a) the customer as a person, (b) the company he works for, (c) the need he has (or details about the enquiry), and (d) the logistics, e.g. when he wants it. This information is also necessary when making appointments, handling enquiries, or any contact where the next sales stage may be handled by someone else. Such informaton may need passing on, writing in the records, or both. Again a formal enquiry form helps.

*A successful sales interview depends on an informed salesman as well as a good product or service.*

Information is gained over many stages, often during the same call as securing an appointment; and the selling process itself can be started at that time. Responding to a customer's enquiry is an ideal opportunity to gain more information, and even if he states his requirements in his enquiry, we can easily ask for more information, as long as it has some bearing on the enquiry.

Similarly, one may make an appointment and then ask for more information; or a request for an interview may follow information gathering. Flexibility is essential. What matters is the information.

There are two main types of information:

1    Information the customer regards as routine and will give quickly and without resistance. This may fall into each category mentioned above (person, company, need etc.) and is best dealt with early in the contact. Included here would be names, addresses, what the company does etc.

2    Information the customer would rather hold until the meeting, or until negotiations have reached a certain stage. This will be more detailed, but could again fall into each category and could cover such things as the level of responsibility of the contact, growth plans of the company, specific applications, re-order prospects, etc.

There is a third type of information which can help salesmen a lot in some situations, and that is information the customer would always be reluctant to divulge — his personal interests, detailed company plans, negotiations with competitors. The salesmen, with experience finds this information 'between the lines', and also by reading the relevant sections of the press, by talking to others in that industry, etc.

*The procedure to secure information*

Initially there are two processes, leading on to a third, later stage:

1    *Asking questions,* in this case usually ones which require more than a yes or no answer. In responding to enquiries, these queries can be direct, but when we approach customers, we have to be a little more circumspect.

2    *Listening.* This must be done carefully, and often with an ear to nuances, hesitations and emphases which could provide the salesman with useful clues. People do not always say what they mean, or mean what they say.

3    *Selection,* that is, matching the facts we have identified to the products that are available, their relevant features, and the benefits which will match the need of the customer. We should also identify the proof that may be necessary to support the situation, such as examples of other applications, precedents, references from other customers, statistics from the Department of Trade, standard specifications etc.

How far we go into this selection stage during the phone call depends on how we assess the enquiry. In the preliminary stages of a complex enquiry we shall not be expected, and not be able, to come up with all the answers, though mentally we may already be doing some selection and framing our end of the conversation accordingly. Selection proper will be desk work to be done after the call. On simpler enquiries, and where we know the answers and responses, we can select as we talk, always remembering that it is far better to call back later, or reserve comment, than to make hurried guesses which may turn out to be wrong.

Whatever call we make, it must be regarded as part of the sales process, with objections being overcome and an aim constantly in sight. It must be assessed as part of the total cycle the customer will go through — often very long and complex — and sometimes it may be a particularly important part of this cycle.

Precisely how we choose to deal with a particular call will depend on the circumstances presented by the customer. Essentially we are often presented with the following choices:

1   The sales office route, from actioning so far as linking to follow-up systems, to selling through the point of order.
2   The support route — setting things up for the representative to follow through and maybe making a specific arrangement.

An example of the progression gone through is shown in Figure 11.1.

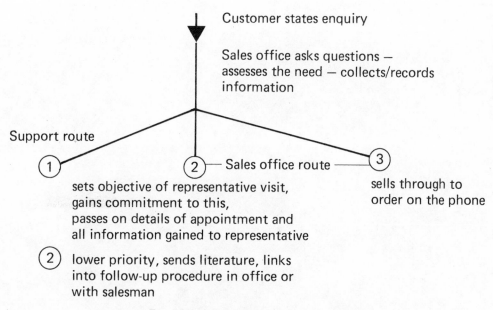

Fig. 11.1 Selecting the course of an enquiry

*Conscious alternatives for low-priority prospects*

What starts out as a support activity may, as we collect information, reveal a low priority-prospect, because of (a) potential order size, (b) timing, (c) special requirements, or (d) usage. Long-term potential is important, but we should be honest and deal with low priorities as such — if necessary resisting requests for a salesman to call in person. Personal selling time is expensive, and should not be wasted on something that can be handled easily by phone or correspondence.

For these prospects, we can proceed as follows:

1   Undertake the complete process there and then on the phone, even saying specifically, if necessary, that a personal visit is not possible.
2   Handle it all by letter, often in liaison with the sales representative concerned, and again emphasising (with apologies) that a call is not possible.
3   Use a combination of telephone and letter.

In every case we should do our best to sell our proposed course of action as a benefit to the customer — less trouble for him and no waiting until a salesman can call.

# Appendix 1:         Telephone Selling

### *Evaluating the need, installing the system*

Most of the organisations that have gone into telephone selling in recent years realise that there is more to the business than just a telephone. While the telephone remains for some a misused, much abused and under-used tool, for others it is a particularly cost-effective selling aid. A survey carried out by Marketing Improvements in 1979 showed that of 108 companies contacted, only 48 per cent had telephone sales departments — a surprising result perhaps in the light of the fact that all these companies could reap substantial benefits from a telephone sales operation.

Telephone selling was pioneered in the UK mainly by companies in the fast-moving consumer goods field and by magazine and newspaper publishers. Probably the most widely advertised operations are those of the *Evening Standard* and *Evening News*, while such companies as Birds Eye, Wrigley and Coca Cola were also among the first to make inroads into this type of selling. Now it is used extensively in many industrial fields as well, in office equipment, plant hire, meat wholesaling, hospital supplies, packing and many more.

Faced with costs, every manager is constantly concerned with analysing sales force costs and seeking ways of reducing them. Latest survey figures (1979) show that the average salesman costs his company around £14,000 per annum (that is, salary, car, commission, operating and management costs). With this in mind, the addition of another salesman to the sales team is hardly the cheapest answer to the problem.

Marketing Improvements' survey shows that the answer for many companies could be telephone selling. As a back-up to the field sales force, this method uses less expensive resources and dramatically reduces the cost per customer contact, while in recent years its methods and techniques have been developed and refined.

### *The potential benefits*

The advantage of this type of activity is that it enables the company to exert much greater control over its sales operations. It can achieve many diverse objectives, far more than just increasing sales. The following are some examples of the kind of objectives that can be set:

1   To increase sales to existing customers against budget.
2   To liberate salesman time by reducing routine calling activity.
3   To increase the frequency of customer contact.
4   To reduce the number of out-of-stock situations in incoming orders compared to solicited orders.
5   To increase the rate at which promotions are sold in.
6   To increase the rate of dissemination of information to customers regarding price, uses, packaging changes, brand activity, etc. (defined by increases in customer contact).
7   To reduce delivery lead time against base period.
8   To open new accounts.
9   To revive moribund accounts which have not ordered for 6 months.
10  To introduce new lines to customers.
11  To negotiate more promotions.
12  To merchandise more effectively (defined by a reduction in requisitions for merchandising material).
13  To increase average order size.
14  To increase the total numbers of orders obtained per week.

As well as the direct effect of the telesales activity, it can free salesmen's time so that more time can be spent on (a) opening new accounts, (b) reviving moribund accounts, (c) selling the full product range, (d) introducing new products, (e) negotiating more promotions, (f) more effective planning etc. Objectives can be set additionally for telesales in transient rather than ongoing situations, e.g. large volume/low profit lines.

### Will it work for you?

Telephone selling seems to work best when most of the following criteria are met with regard to:

1   *The customers.* They must be prepared to accept, or able to be persuaded to accept, coming to the telephone, and be accessible by this medium of communication.
    They will usually be handling large numbers of competitive products with limitations on storage and cash so that stock levels are an important factor in running their business.
2   *The products.* The products must be well known to the customers so that a general awareness can be assumed. If not, telephone conversations will become long drawn out, with expensive explanations about the product and its performance, frequently ending up with a request by the customer to see the salesman anyway.
    The products will normally be of the fast-moving, non-durable consumer type.
    The average order unit value will usually be quite high.
    Ideally physical stock checks should not be necessary before the placing of an order.
3   *The sales force.* The number of actual or potential accounts per salesman will be high (100+).
    Calls will be made at regular intervals (while they can vary from once a week to twice a year, accounts with low call frequencies do not respond as well as more active accounts).
    The sales force will usually be expected to set a wide product range and undertake a range of activities.

*How to go about it*

Telephone selling should not be regarded as a tool which can be used either to replace the sales force or as a cost-cutting means of reducing its size. It works most effectively and efficiently when co-ordinated and integrated with existing sales activities. To be successful, therefore, an active telephone selling operation might best be installed in a systematic way based upon the following steps.

## Step 1    Define the objectives

Objectives should be stated in clear and measurable terms so that the results achieved can be assessed and congruence with the company's marketing objectives ensured. To start such an operation without precise objectives is to predispose it to failure and decay. It is also worth stressing that there are always company politicians who are adept at either recommending that there should be no objectives or at writing opaque, failure-based ones — consciously or, worse, unconsciously. Precise targets need to be set for order sizes, conversion rates for telephone calls, number of calls to be made in a set period and so on.

## Step 2    Planning and controls

The volume of sales by product to be sold and the types of customer to be sold to should be planned. So should the frequency of customer contact; and the role of the telephone selling system in relation to the outside sales force should be defined. Existing paperwork and order-processing systems need to be assessed and any changes needed made so that the telesales operation is compatible with these, and communications within the company are able to flow smoothly.

## Step 3    Recruitment and selection

The recruitment and selection of competent personnel to operate the teleselling are important but difficult. It is unwise and a false economy to assume that teleselling can be undertaken by 'any old spare and under-occupied member of staff'. Telephone selling demands talented and very specialised staff. There are specific skills that must either be possessed or developed by training. There are also basic problems of mental attitude which must be acknowledged if the operation is to be successful. Much of the advice given in my colleague John Lidstone's excellent book *Recruiting and Selecting Successful Salesmen* is relevant to this special category of sales staff.

## Step 4    Sell the idea to the sales force

It is essential to sell the idea to the salesmen to ensure their active co-operation from the outset. Salesmen live in conditions of uncertainty, so are naturally both wary and tend to feel insecure when changes are sprung upon them. Initially they are somewhat special, particularly because they will have to nominate and submit worth-while accounts to be phoned. This is important. If salesmen are not consulted on this aspect, the operation will start off with built-in competition from the sales force. Indeed, more than one new operation has faltered in the early stages because salesmen were persuading customers not to use the telephone sales service. The salesmen should be told why the company is introducing telephone selling: the benefits it will bring for them, what is expected of them, what changes it will make to their jobs, and the timetable of actions to be taken.

When recruited, the telephone sales operator(s) should accompany a cross-section of salesmen making normal customer calls as part of their training. This will reassure the salesmen that these operators are conversant at first hand with the customers, what they look like, what their needs are, what they buy, and what they do with the products.

*Step 5    Sell the idea to the customers*

It is a vital preliminary to achieve customer co-operation and identification with the new system. Customers should be sold the benefits of the telephone selling, preferably by the salesman on an individual basis.

*Step 6    Implement and validate*

Like any other marketing or sales tool, telephone selling should be tested on a pilot basis before a company goes 'national' or commits all its resources to it. Its 'testability' over reasonably short periods is one of the factors that make it an attractive technique to experiment with. Initially a controlled implementation should follow the plans drawn up in Step 2. The pilot test should last long enough to provide data on all the variables that could arise, to allow for seasonal fluctuations and to enable a pattern and volume of sales results to be obtained.

*Summary*

Telephone selling can have a positive impact on many aspects of a company's sales operation. However, perhaps it is wise to end this section with a final word of warning to companies contemplating setting up an active telephone sales operation. It must be started for the right reasons — to sell to the right people at the right time and using the right type of trained personnel. There are innumerable stories of companies which thought that all telephone selling consisted of was a desk, a chair, a telephone and any spare, unoccupied member of the staff.

# Part Four

# Maintaining an Effective Inside Sales Team

# 12: Development and Appraisal

Development and appraisal are a direct responsibility of management, and can never be abandoned or delegated. They may be time-consuming, but since they are among management's main functions, there can be no excuse for 'lack of time'. Development must be a continuous cycle (Figure 12.1), planned right from the day of recruitment and progressed as the person's needs, ability and potential are identified, against known job requirements. To control this process, there must be formal standards. *Job descriptions* are essential for both management and employee to know what is required in the job, and effective methods of *appraisal* and *assessment* are necessary to evaluate performance.

We have already looked at job descriptions (pp.22, 25), and their importance is reflected by the requirement in current employment legislation for every person to have a job description (against which, among other things, most unfair dismissal proceedings are judged). Rightly enough, it is argued that no one can be judged to be doing a job properly if there is no adequate description of the job.

The growth of 'white collar' unions means that more and more sales offices are becoming unionised, and job descriptions have become a fundamental part of practically all negotiations between unions and management.

Appraisal and assessment are essential if development is to be a continuous process. Assessment forms can be a major help, especially where there is a fairly large staff, not because the manager cannot see everyone as an individual, but as an aid to comparing a number of people doing very similar jobs. Assessment forms should be tailor-made according to the requirements and functions of the particular jobs, though many elements, such as attitude to colleagues/seniors/juniors, punctuality, enthusiasm, etc. are common to all jobs. The example in Figure 12.2 may be useful as a basis for an assessment form.

### Appraisal meetings

In some companies there may not be a formal appraisal and development system organised by the personnel department; then it is the job of each manager to arrange this for his own staff. But generally, though appraisals may be done in conjunction with the personnel department,

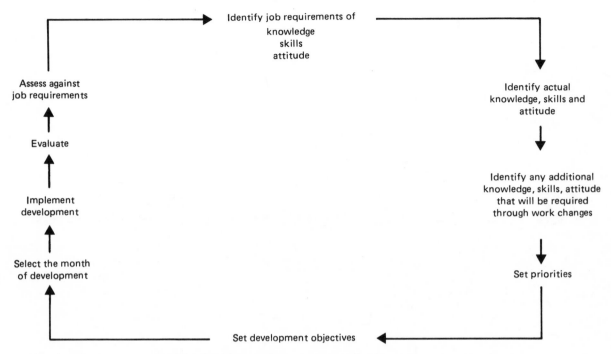

**Fig. 12.1 The continuous cycle of development**

they should never be handed over to the personnel department for them to deal with alone. In many cases managers arrange separate appraisal meetings in addition to the formal 'company' assessment.

Appraisal meetings should take place at least once and preferably twice a year (especially for more junior staff, whose job does not revolve so much around the company year), and they should be opportunities for individual members of the staff to have unhurried, constructive and confidential discussions with their managers about all aspects of the job. Some companies allow a third person to be present if the staff member wishes it — a staff association representative, a shop steward — or for the meeting to be held with the person to whom the (appraising) manager himself is responsible.

The three most important things to remember about conducting appraisal meetings are preparation, sufficient time, and confidentiality.

*Preparation*

The manager must be prepared to discuss the job itself, prospects, salary, performance and training. It is no use opening the person's file five minutes before he is due. The manager must give the members of his staff plenty of time to prepare as well — there should be a specific month when appraisals are carried out, and individual dates should be fixed a month or so in advance.

*Time*

Allocate enough time. A person's life and career are being discussed, and they should not be rushed. In addition, it should be undisturbed time — if necessary hold the interviews away from the office to ensure there are no interruptions.

JOB HOLDER'S NAME:                                      DATE:

JOB TITLE:

ASSESSOR'S NAME:


ASSESSMENT OF KEY TASKS:

| KEY TASKS | RESULTS ACHIEVED against performance standards | ASSESSMENT |
|---|---|---|
|  |  |  |

What is your overall assessment of Job Holder's performance?

What are his strengths?

His areas for improvement

Rating:    Outstanding ☐                    Average ☐
           Above average ☐          Needs training and improvements ☐
                                     Poor ☐

**Fig. 12.2 Example of assessment form**

What specific training and experience does the job holder need in the next 12 months?

2.

3.

ACTION

- Arrange the next meeting
- Has the job changed since the last appraisal? If any of the Key Tasks or Performance Standards are inappropriate then redraft them on the Action Plan.
- Complete Action Plan

Comments by Assessor's Senior

Signed .................................... Date ..........................

Assessor's Signature ........................................ Date ..........................

Job Holder's Comments

Signed .................................... Date ..........................

**Fig. 12.2 (cont.)**

*Confidentiality*

Everyone should feel they can speak their minds without what they say being held against them. A staff member who is apprehensive about discussing his job, his performance and his expectations will soon stop caring. Besides, good managers should not be put off by criticism, even from their juniors.

The important points agreed at the meeting must be summarised in writing and approved by the person concerned as soon as possible. Remember to *live up to promises* made in the interview.

*Training*

Having identified any development needs and priorities, the management's next responsibility is to select the best method of training. Development means continuously learning more and being responsible for more complex tasks, and training is obviously an integral part of development. In many companies there will be a training officer or co-ordinator within the personnel department, and managers will be able to call on him in planning individual training requirements.

Training can be either *formal* or *informal.*

Formal training means specified periods of pure instruction, following a predetermined pattern and sequence. Formal courses can be run by a company's management or training department or outside specialists and may be held during working hours or at special weekend or evening courses. Standard induction courses are frequently conducted by companies, and many of them are for new arrivals in all divisions, but, after that, training courses will need to be designed for specific activities.

Managers and company training departments make frequent use of outside sources for training, sending individuals or small groups of staff on courses run by many of the specialist course and seminar organisations or consultants. These courses usually are able to offer a degree of professionalism of content and presentation which companies themselves may not match.

Informal training should go on all the time, and should range from the 'sit by Nelly' technique of learning by example to planned periods of brief instruction followed by learning through experience, the 'subject' spending increasing periods working without supervision. Informal 'on the job' training is often more effective than formal courses, but it must be properly prepared. 'Sit by Nelly' is only a suitable technique if 'Nelly' is doing her job properly and is not going to gossip, pass rumours, and explain all the unofficial tricks of the trade for hoodwinking managers and silencing awkward customers. And 'Nelly' should be able to give lucid explanations about all she is doing.

The appointed training supervisor must never be too far away during informal training. Doing something 'for real' is better than make-believe, but it can be full of anxiety for a first-timer. While being thrown in at the deep end can teach many to swim, it can also cost lives if help is not nearby. We should always be ready to be 'rescuers' of the people we are training.

The manager himself may delegate some detailed instructions to another member of his staff (as in 'sit by Nelly'), but he must still oversee operations, keep an eye on progress, and make certain that 'Nelly' is clear about what has to be taught and how long the trainee is to remain an observer. Since showing someone the ropes and instructing them is disruptive of normal routine, the manager may have to make arrangements for the instructor to have extra help with his or her usual workload.

When training, no matter how simple or complex the task, we should always ensure that:

1 The person under training understands the subject completely.
2 An explanation of the tasks, and how they fit into the rest of the operation, is given.
3 A description of the tasks is provided.
4 If complex, a demonstration, part by part and then in total, is given.
5 The chance to practise under guidance is afforded.
6 The trainee then does the work above, but has somewhere to refer to (a colleague, a manager or to the operations manual) when in doubt.

Failure to brief comprehensively and in context often causes problems, e.g. someone preparing quotations may be shown exactly how to do so, but if they are not aware of the function of such quotations as part of the sales process their attitude and commitment to the task may be purely 'administrative' and the result not as effective as possible.

Development does not only rely entirely on training, however, and simply experiencing different work is just as important a part of development. But it has to be done in measured stages, and it is the manager's job to gauge when to expose someone in his staff to new experiences. Too early an exposure could harm the company and weaken the person's confidence. Too late an exposure could lead to a bored, dissatisfied employee leaving for another, more challenging job.

In a sales office, where there are a large number of different activities, many of which are very brief and intermittent, one of the key ways in which we can ensure that those below us develop, gain experience, extend their skills, and so become more valuable, is by delegation.

# 13:                                          *Delegation*

Let us be clear, delegation is more than simply work allocation. We can define it as 'the art and act of giving a subordinate the necessary authority to make decisions for us in a specified area of *our* work'. So it has more permanent implications.

When we delegate, we pass responsibility to our subordinate, and give him adequate authority to take appropriate decisions. The handing over of authority as well as responsibility is extremely important, and failure to do so is a common mistake.

Some people delegate with ease. Witness a memo received by a training manager from one department head in answer to a request that he should attend a training session on delegation, which read: 'I will not be able to attend myself — but will send my assistant.'

Many managers, however, are very reluctant to delegate, often because they think that giving authority to someone else, a subordinate, weakens their own position. But a manager who never delegates cannot develop a team, and instead of becoming a leader of an effective team, grows into a dictator over a disgruntled staff, his department's achievement limited by the amount of activity he can undertake. Teamwork to some managers is a question of 'lots of people doing what I say'.

We cannot delegate to an individual work that is already part of his function and within his job description. We can only delegate work that is legitimately our own but is a logical extension of the other person's activities. Ideally it should be related to developing that person's skills, and not simply a way of giving ourselves an easier time.

In giving someone else the authority to act on our behalf we must accept that we are at the same time giving them the 'right' to be wrong. Delegation, therefore, supposes not only the essential element of mutual trust but also some element of risk.

*The benefits of delegation*

Carefully thought out and responsible delegation has the following benefits:

1    It provides real opportunity to develop skills and experience in subordinates, thus motivating individuals through achievement and personal growth.

115

2     It allows the manager to concentrate time and effort on aspects of his job which are keys to the efficiency and success of the operation.

3     It generates interest and stimulates morale through the department/team.

4     It allows the manager to stand back from the daily rush and routine, and to think and plan creatively for the future.

*Reducing the risks of delegating*

There are clearly a number of risks in delegating. We may judge the subordinate incorrectly and delegate the wrong responsibility to the wrong person. Their inability to deal with it properly, the mistakes they make, may cause considerable disruption and perhaps lost revenue or increased expenditure.

If things go wrong as a consequence of our delegating, we may have to 'carry the can' and pick up the pieces for someone else's errors. Inevitably we will sometimes be blamed by our seniors for taking the wrong delegating decision.

We can reduce the risks by the following means:

1     Avoiding delegating the wrong kinds of job, such as:
   (a)   matters essential to overall control,
   (b)   discipline,
   (c)   policy deviation (do not experiment *and* delegate),
   (d)   confidential matters,
   (e)   grievance settlements.

2     Choosing the most suitable person. We should ask ourselves:
   (a)   has he done something similar before?
   (b)   how much knowledge has he shown about this?
   (c)   has he shown signs of being able to take such decisions?
   (d)   is he likely to be acceptable to others affected?
   (e)   is the job too complex? Is training needed before delegation is sensible? What form could this training take?

3     Communicating fully to the following:
   (a)   the individual,
   (b)   his colleagues,
   (c)   other managers, if affected,
   (d)   more senior management, if affected.

Lack of communication is a common cause of the delegation process going wrong. We must make sure that everyone knows that we have trust in our deputy's ability to decide and act. We must also make sure that everyone knows the degree of authority we have delegated — leaving blurred lines of authority and responsibility can disrupt the whole exercise. Above all, we should ensure that the individual knows why the job is necessary, and why we have asked *him* to do it.

In explaining this, we should also make it clear whether this is a trial delegation, a 'one off' step, or part of his development and, subject to his succeeding, a permanent responsibility which will be written into his job description. Additional renumeration will have to be discussed if responsibilities are to be increased permanently.

4     Monitoring progress. This is always difficult, for we have to be careful not to interfere or appear to be going back on our decision to delegate. Yet we must also keep in contact with what is happening so that we can give guidance, remembering that the subordinate's decisions and methods may be different in approach, yet in the end be equally correct, and that we have given him the authority to do it his way.

Right at the beginning we should, if possible, notify the individual of the standards we require, and show him how he, too, can monitor his results, perhaps building in stages where he can check with us rather than us with him. Above all, we should have the patience to resist all temptations to take back a task ourselves, unless we are positive that the subordinate is unwittingly heading for disaster; even then we should suggest, drop a hint, make a recommendation, rather than adopt a 'Here, let me do that' attitude of superiority.

### Evaluating the results of delegation

Even if we delegated a responsibility with the intention of it becoming a permanent transfer, there should always be a period after which we review the subordinate's handling of his extra or new task (he, in turn, may have been able to hand on down the line some of his previous activities). This should not take place too soon. We should try to recollect the way we learnt the job ourselves, remembering that we tend to flatter ourselves when recalling our abilities.

The questions we need to ask in evaluating results include the following:

1 Has a new way of doing the job emerged, and might it bring wider benefits if applied throughout the section or the company? We must force ourselves to consider whether the job may not only be done differently to the way we have gone about it in the past, but better.
2 Has the subordinate shown himself to be capable of easily accepting responsibilities and authority? Could he accept more?
3 Are there other tasks we are still handling which we could delegate?
4 Has the success of the venture stimulated others in the team to want more responsibility?
5 Have any other functions suffered as a result? Does the subordinate have enough time to complete his work properly?
6 Should we be talking with our manager about updating job descriptions to transfer permanently some delegated tasks to subordinates?
7 How much of our time has been saved? And are we using that time to good advantage?

If it is obvious that the delegation has been less than a success, we should try to find out why, rather than suspect that 'the only way to do something properly is to do it myself'. We should ask ourselves more questions, as follows:

1 What was the main thing that went wrong? Why specifically was it not a success?
2 What are the causes of that?
3 What did we do wrong?
4 Have we made time to analyse what exactly went wrong, and to learn from our mistake?
5 Could the same delegation have worked with different preparation/different people?

### Conclusion

The decisions people carry out with the greatest enthusiasm are those they take themselves. Even if the person makes a wrong decision, if it is his own, he will, more often than not, turn it into a right one through sheer effort. Allowing people to make more decisions for themselves, and so work more enthusiastically, depends on delegation.

Deciding on what can be delegated and then having the determination to do it requires a great deal of conscious effort (and often sacrifice — we may have to delegate some of the responsibilities that we enjoy the most). It is not easy to give people the right to be wrong when we will be accountable for the mistakes that are made; but the risks are worth the rewards in terms of (a) our own effectiveness, (b) the opportunity to motivate, (c) the growth in personal ability of our staff and of ourselves.

Let us ask ourselves what sort of manager we like to report to, one who delegates or one who does not. That helps us form a view of how our team will regard — and respond — to us in this respect.

# 14:                                  *Motivation*

Motivation is concerned with understanding people's internal needs and emotions (what causes them to act in a certain way) and with creating a situation that ensures they want to put as much as they can into their work. Nearly all the eventually useless and often harmful 'motivational plans' which abound in sales organisation stem from ignorance of what actually 'makes people tick'; an understanding of people and what their internal needs are is essential if we are to manage effectively. No matter how well organised everything else is, an unmotivated staff can never get good results.

There are hundreds of books and articles about human behaviour and job motivation. (Much of my colleague John Lidstone's excellent book *Motivating Your Sales Force* would provide a further reference relevant to the sales office and its personnel.) But it is one thing to theorise about motivation, and quite another to practise it successfully. We can, however, easily pick up enough of the basic principles to improve the way we perform as managers and leaders considerably.

In a sales office our principle resource is our people. Having recruited them, we have a responsibility to get the best out of them. This means taking into account their individual personalities, the job they are doing, and their place in the team. Most importantly, it means that we should create and maintain the most favourable 'environment', physical and emotional, in which effort and achievement can flourish, for the team, for each individual, and for the company.

We all know people who profess to know instinctively what makes other people tick, and who are supremely confident of their ability to get the best out of them. Usually they are very wide of the mark.

There are two overriding principles behind successful motivation. First, it must be *continuous*. Maintaining a good motivational atmosphere in a group needs constant thought and attention. There are no panaceas, and often it is the cumulative effect of continuous care and attention to the problem that brings results. Second, it must be *individual*. There is no particular reason why what is important to or 'turns on' one person should be regarded similarly by another. The successful man-managers treat every person as an individual, know what sort of things do drive people in general, and try to relate these factors to individuals in particular cases. They also query their handling of others — only in that way can they ensure that they are treating job attitudes as personal, individual emotions. Only individual approaches can achieve the proper motivational balance. Further a censorious view that says 'why are they so concerned about this?', 'surely that cannot be upsetting them', or equally 'this must surely excite them', sets the scene for serious miscalculation in motivation.

## Aspects of motivation

There are two quite separate but interdependent aspects of motivation, much of whose terminology was 'coined' by Frederick Herzberg. (His book *Work and the Nature of Man*, published in 1968, gave rise to much of the subsequent thinking on this subject.) The aspects are:

1  The environment in which the job is performed, which produces either satisfaction or dissatisfaction, but tends more often to produce the latter (or at least is not noticed one way of the other). Because they more often cause dissatisfaction than satisfaction, the job environment factors are known as negative motivators, dissatisfiers (or hygiene factors).
2  The job itself and the emotions caused by it.

Positive motivation in the form of satisfiers (or motivating factors) is more likely to come from the job itself. Yet, almost traditionally, the job environment gets more attention from unenlightened management looking to improve motivation.

In motivation, it is the balance that is important. If none of the potential dissatisfiers is actually aggravating a job holder, and if none of the positive motivators is at work either, then motivationally he is 'in neutral'!

The absence of dissatisfiers, or the removal of previously present dissatisfiers by management does not create motivation, but only prevents dissatisfaction. However, this is important, for it can create an environment in which the positive motivators can work.

So, in practice, the real sum of motivation is *motivators* minus *dissatisfiers*. By looking at the two separately, we can identify the practical steps to take as managers to achieve a constant positive motivational balance. The various factors and their relationship with either positive or negative motivational effect are demonstrated in the form Herzberg described, in Figure 14.1, and comments then follow about each factor in turn.

## Dissatisfiers

### Company policy and administration

Problems arise in the following circumstances:

1  A person feels that company policy and procedures conflict with his personal aims.
2  Policies and procedures are not explained in terms of benefit to the individual — one of the most common dissatisfiers because tasks eventually seem irrelevant or meaningless, and doing meaningless tasks in a robot-like manner is extremely discouraging.

### Supervision

This may produce the following dissatisfactions:

1  A person may feel that supervision is intrusive, 'policing', dictatorial, etc.
2  There may seem to be no benefit accruing from the supervision, no link with training and development, etc.

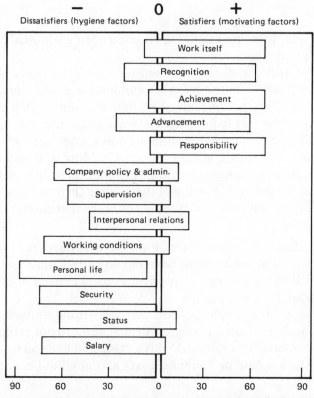

Fig. 14.1 Herzberg's satisfiers and dissatisfiers

## Interpersonal relations

These can cause much dissatisfaction, because of unfair, unreasonable superiors; unco-operative or back-stabbing equals; difficult, sniping subordinates; or any combination of them all. Friction arises when people within the same operation seem to be pulling in different directions, or when a person feels he is being discriminated against.

## Working conditions

Office location and layout, office furnishing, telephone facilities, company cars, etc. can all cause problems if they are not felt to be adequate, or do not reflect the importance and status of the job. Petty rules with no logical basis cause much dissatisfaction.

Most difficulties and dissatisfactions stem from comparison rather than the working conditions themselves. Someone else, or equivalent people in another company, has a better office, an individual office rather than a drab open-plan, a larger car, a personal telephone, etc.

## Status

As we are all members of a society and of various social groups, we are all conscious of our status within them. The three principal groups within which we perceive our status are the work group, the family group, and the social group. Considerable unhappiness and anxiety are created if a person feels his status in any of these groups is threatened, for the urge to 'belong' is a very powerful instinct in mankind. Worries in this area may not, however, be openly expressed very easily.

*Security*

The need for security is far more prevalent than is often openly admitted. People have a deep-seated need to feel safe and secure.

But because, like cowardice and fear, the need for security is rarely bluntly stated, many managers (who may themselves enjoy a sense of considerable security) tend to forget or ignore its importance to others. We should remember, too, that quite often those who have the greatest need for security often try to pretend otherwise in what they say, and in their attitudes.

The need for security makes itself felt in many ways, and many of the factors already described are also likely to distort a person's security, adding to their unease. Uncertainty, ambiguities, rumours, sudden changes (even the most minor change, such as rearranging an office layout) can upset people by disturbing or threatening their security.

Therefore, in considering this factor, we should always bear in mind that people's security is strengthened by the following:

1 *Clarity.* Clear, uncomplicated instructions are necessary, not vague statements or ambiguous orders. The job we want done should be explained clearly and simply, and what we want done laid down in precise terms. The person must be given every opportunity to ask for clarification.

2 *Strong leadership.* Most employees will welcome strong leadership. The majority of those doing jobs that do not have a great deal of authority or responsibility will prefer someone who will say, 'You should do this' or 'I would like you to do that', rather than 'Do what you think is best' or 'I suppose that's all right, but I'm not sure. What do you think?'

3 *Structure.* People prefer to work within a framework of rules rather than be left to find their own way, though the rules must be sensible and relevant, and explained to the people who have to obey them. Specifically, staff need to know (a) precise and definitive statements of duties, responsibilities and scope of authority; and (b) the number of activities to be carried out, the types of business to be developed, quotas to be achieved etc.; and to be given some definition of the quality of work to be achieved.

4 *Belonging.* Nearly all of us prefer to belong to a team or community than to be a lone wolf. Making staff feel that they are part of a team is important, and they should be brought together as often as circumstances permit. A sporting analogy adds an important dimension here to the team concept. Most people who belong to (or support) a team want it to do well, to be the best team. It follows logically that it is in fact easier to manage in a situation where we set high standards, and go for being best, than by being lax and letting things slide.

5 *Being kept informed.* Secrecy allows rumours to start and spread, threatening security. We should always tell employees as much as possible — formally, informally, and even through the 'grapevine'.

*Salary*

As far as motivation is concerned, there is a great difference between absolute salary level and a salary increase. Salary level is part of the working environment, and is a potential dissatisfier. It is never enough, it is always lower than someone else's, another firm always pays more, etc. A salary increase, however, is seen as recognition for achievement and as such is a potential motivator (whereas a fixed yearly increment is simply part of an absolute salary level). But today's increase rapidly becomes tomorrow's normal salary, and the motivational effect soon wears off.

Some managers believe that all their motivational problems would be solved if only the 'right' remuneration scheme could be constructed, but there is widespread belief, and considerable evidence, that pay is relatively unimportant (after a certain level of need, rather than desire) provided that other incentives are applied. There are thousands of examples, e.g. in small engineering companies, where skilled or semi-skilled workers would not think of crossing the road to a car assembly plant even though they could increase their pay substantially by doing so. Many salesman, too, prefer to sell particular types of product, even though the financial rewards are less.

Nevertheless, pay is important, and it is vital when it is:

1 Below subsistence level.
2 Below habitual living standards.
3 Seems to be unfair in comparison with others doing the same work under the same conditions. This often occurs in situations where salesmen receive a generous commission or bonus, while the inside sales people, who might contribute significantly to their sales, do not; or where an examination of salaries alone can identify the prettiest secretaries.

## Motivators

### Achievement

For an individual to see that he has achieved something, he must have a standard or an objective against which he can measure his achievement. Success is relative: to run a mile in 6 minutes may be an achievement, or it may not, depending on the standard by which the runner is measured, or measures himself. It may be fast enough to win the race, or so slow that he comes last. He might have achieved his personal best time, or it might tell him he is way off form.

It is important, therefore, for standards to be set and communicated to the individual, and for a system of measurement to be devised — though this need not be a stifling, rigid set of targets. Achievement must be engineered within each individual's job, and it must be recognised.

### Recognition

It is not enough for a person to know he has achieved something; for we have a desire for others to recognise and appreciate our achievement. Recognition is not something that a manager gives out of the kindness of his heart. It is something a person earns and deserves by achievement of objectives, by doing something extra, by the application of intelligent effort.

Recognition is essentially a personal thing, and is best conveyed orally. A spoken word of thanks or praise from a superior does more for motivation than a standard letter from the highest, remotest level of the company. Depending on the degree of achievement, that oral recognition can be strengthened in the following ways:

1 Further oral recognition in front of other people (praise in public, criticise in private).
2 Written recognition: a letter from a director or the chairman, a memorandum, a mention in the company newspaper, a bulletin on the notice board etc.
3 A token reward, e.g. a meal at a restaurant, a gift voucher, theatre tickets, flowers etc. are often better motivators than a bonus cheque for the same amount.
4 A salary increase.
5 A payment through an incentive scheme (though incentive schemes, including one-off schemes, need to be very carefully thought out to prevent them being dissatisfiers to some who may feel they have a more difficult job).

Incentive schemes, which can be based on many factors apart from money, including gifts, coupons, travel etc., offer tangible recognition. If they are to have an effect, they must:

1   Be judged on results, (a) relating directly to an activity for which an individual is responsible, or (b) relating directly to factors over which the individual has control.
2   Encompass a large volume of activity (or orders) to get over any freak effects.
3   Represent a reward worth having, worth making the extra effort to achieve.
4   Be simple, straightforward and easy to understand.
5   Have payment made promptly, i.e. soon after the effort that earned it.

Clearly a meagre reward paid long after the event and on a scheme too complicated for people easily to calculate 'how they are doing so far' is unlikely to have much impact.

These, we should always remember, are reinforcements of verbal recognition, and should not be seen as substitutes.

A slightly different aspect of recognition is often called 'feedback'. This may not revolve round achievement or over-achievement, but prevents the sensation of working in a vacuum. Feedback is answering or responding to memos that may not really require a reply, saying 'Thank you' for information passed through a third party, commenting on persons doing something which is not always part of their function, passing on compliments received from customers, and keeping the sales office informed about negotiations or any other situation they have played a part in. Feedback is recognition that a person exists as a human being with emotions and desires.

### Work itself

Work in itself is a motivator. It is easier and more enjoyable to be busy than to be bored, and despite everyone's grumbles, twentieth-century Western man does want to work.

The one great condition governing this is that the work should seem to be meaningful. It is management's job to give purpose and direction to a job. This can be done by setting and communicating the right objectives to employees, and by explaining the objectives in terms of the objectives of the whole company.

Nevertheless there is a lot of work that can hardly ever be anything but dull and routine and, on the face of it, have little apparent use in relation to time and effort. Management should appreciate that this work is usually more difficult than stimulating and creative work, and should compensate by giving added recognition and responsibility to those tasks. Habitually, however, we reserve recognition and responsibility for those jobs which are already motivationally rewarding, which further adds to the frustation of tedious jobs.

Many 'menial' jobs can be given extra appeal by personalising them, enhancing recognition by allowing people to sign their own names to outgoing correspondence, or by dividing a number of routine tasks so that each person deals with various stages of, for instance, processing an order, rather than have each group dealing with only one stage. A car assembly line (in many ways conceptually little different from some clerical functions in large companies) is tedious work because everyone works in isolation, with no sense of achievement. No one on an assembling line has any sense of actually building a car, because they carry out only one function. In a different system, groups of individuals carry out a large number of different tasks towards an identifiable end.

### Responsibility

Many managers find it easier to give reasons why a subordinate's weaknesses make him unsuitable for responsibility than to look for strengths which would enable him to take responsibility. Giving responsibility is an essential part of development, and we have already seen that this is a major managerial function. With few exceptions, people do look for responsibility, and very often the person concerned is the best judge of when responsibility is too heavy for him.

Responsibility can take many forms and stages: the person can take responsibility for his own actions by signing letters, he may be made more responsible by removing some supervision, or by making him check his own figures rather than have this done by a supervisor. Responsibility does not always mean being in control of others.

The giving of responsibility should be discussed with the person concerned, and they should be clear about what it means. Generally it will be welcomed, for it shows that we believe in their strengths, and are attempting to develop them in their job.

*Advancement*

Advancement can be divided into two types:

1    The development of the person's abilities within the job.
2    Personal growth and promotion — often into other jobs.

There is satisfaction in the awareness that what we are doing now is more important, or is done better than what we were doing a year ago. No one wants to be on a treadmill, but everyone can enjoy a walk.

A sense of advancement is a direct result of a proper development programme, even if promotion is a long time coming. The company that has very few levels of advancement creates problems for itself, because it inhibits a proper development programme, making far too many people compete for too few positions. Nevertheless false status positions should be avoided, for their motivation will be short-lived. In many companies the pace of change is such, often in response to the market, that many jobs can be developed in this kind of way.

Promotion can be in part a recognition of previous development, but a sense of advancement can equally come from frequent recognition, from attending training courses, from changing jobs (at the same level, which increases experience and therefore worth), from salary rises, by being called on for advice, by being brought into meetings, etc. Training is a key area in motivation, showing that we recognise a person's abilities, making them aware that they have achieved recognition and expertise, enriching their jobs by broadening their experience and increasing their abilities, giving them the responsibility of justifying the investment in them by training, and also giving them a sense of advancement by learning new abilities, by development and promotion.

There is a timing factor that must always be borne in mind when making adjustments to the motivational balance. Figure 14.2 shows how attitude, activity and results respond to positive or negative inputs.

Understanding what motivates people in their work, and positively controlling these factors, both on the positive and negative sides, must result in a more effective sales office. The factor which perhaps sums up everything that is important in this whole area of maintaining an effective and enthusiastic sales team is leadership. In considering this we can, first, perhaps usefully consider what people look for ideally in their 'best' (not most likeable) manager compared with that they get. Many common factors emerge when people are asked about this (see Figure 14.3, reproduced from *Motivating Your Sales Force*).

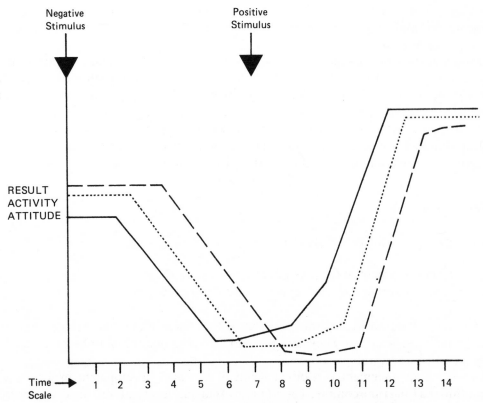

Fig. 14.2 Time relationship of impacts on motivational balance

| Qualities expected from a manager: | What they too often experience: a manager who: |
|---|---|
| 1 *Fairness* - does not have pets and favourites. | 1 Is a 'yes-man' to his superiors. |
| 2 *Decisiveness* - not afraid to make decisions, however unpopular. | 2 Is a 'no-man' to me. |
| 3 *Loyalty* - takes responsibility himself when things go wrong. | 3 Passes off the ideas of others as his own. |
| 4 *Expertise* - can do what he asks us to do. | 4 Stabs others in the back. |
| 5 *Honesty* - gives sincere praise and criticism. | 5 Gets rid of anyone who threatens him. |
| 6 *Courage* - gets rid of dead wood, tells top management the truth. | 6 Passes the buck when he makes mistakes. |
| 7 *Humanity* - treats me as a human being. | 7 Manipulates the facts to his own advantage. |
| 8 *Good delegator* - shares objectives with me. | 8 Blackmails me into compliance. |
| 9 *Consistency* - I know where I stand. | |

Fig. 14.3 The ideal/real manager

Second, we can usefully spend a moment thinking about some of the factors that contribute to leadership and make it work. No apology, therefore, for including, as Appendix 2, notes based on the work of John Adair, whose book *Training for Leadership* is fully identified on p.138 which lists suggested further reading.

# *Appendix 2:*                  *Leadership*

Your effectiveness as a leader depends on your ability to influence and be influenced by your department in the implementation of a common task.

You must:

1   Ensure continuous *task* achievement
2   Meet the *needs of your group*
3   Meet the *needs of individual group members.*

These three areas interact with each other as shown in Figure A.1. This overlapping means that neglect of any one has a considerable influence on the performance in the other two areas. The significance of this relationship can be checked by listing the *action* you must take under each area.

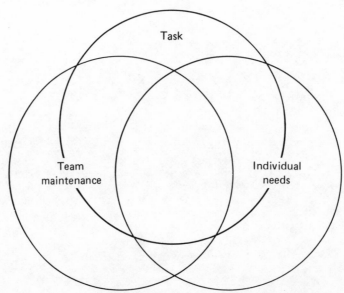

**Fig. A.1 Interaction of areas in effective leadership**

### A.1   Achieving the task

You must avoid the temptation to 'do it yourself'. Your most effective contribution to achieving the required results lies in:

1   Being clear what the task is.
2   Understanding how it fits into the overall short- and long-term objectives of the company.
3   Planning how you will accomplish it.
4   Defining and providing the resources needed, including time and authority.
5   Doing all you can to ensure that the department structure allows the task to be done effectively.
6   Controlling progress during the completion of the task.
7   Evaluating results and comparing them with the original objective set.

*Checklist for achieving the task*

1   Am I clear about my own responsibilities and authority?
2   Am I clear about my department objectives — have I agreed them with my boss?
3   Have I worked out a programme for reaching these objectives?
4   Can the job be restructured to get better results?
5   Are the physical working conditions right for the job?
6   Does everyone know and has everyone agreed what his targets and performance standards are (including myself)?
7   Are there any gaps in the abilities of the group?
8   Am I aware of how my team and I are spending our time? Is it the best way? Are our priorities right?
9   When it is necessary for me to be involved in the work, do I ensure that the team is managed as effectively as before?
10   Am I receiving regular records which enable me to monitor progress?
11   What arrangements do I make for continuity of management in my absence?
12   Do I periodically take stock? Have I achieved my tasks? If not, why not?
13   Do my standards of work and behaviour set the best possible example to the group?

### A.2   Meeting individual needs

Each individual within a working group must:

1   Feel a sense of personal achievement in the job and that his contribution is worth while.
2   Feel that the job itself is challenging, is demanding the best of him and is giving responsibility to match his capability.
3   Receive adequate recognition for his achievements.
4   Have control over those aspects of his job for which he is accountable.
5   Feel that he as an individual is advancing in experience and ability.

*Checklist for meeting individual needs*

Providing the right climate and opportunities for individual needs to be met is your most difficult yet also your most challenging and rewarding task.

For each member of the team ask yourself these questions:

1   Have I agreed responsibilities (results) and performance standards with him?
2   Has he a continuing list of agreed short-term targets for improvement?
3   Does he have the resources (including authority) to achieve agreed standards?
4   Have I made adequate provision for training?
5   In the event of success do I acknowledge it and build on it? In the case of failure do I criticise constructively and give guidance?
6   Does the individual see some pattern of career development?
7   Can I remove some controls though still retain my accountability? Can I cut down on the amount of checking and hold him more and more responsible for his own quality and accuracy?
8   Can I increase the individual's accountability for his own work?
9   Can I give additional authority? Could queries on his subject be made to him instead of me?
10   Is his overall performance regularly reviewed with him?
11   Is his pay in balance with his capacity?
12   Does he need relocation in a job more closely matching his capacity if after training he still fails to achieve the required standards?
13   Do I know enough about each individual to enable me to have an accurate picture of his needs? Do I really know how he feels about things?
14   Do I give sufficient time and personal attention to matters of direct concern to each individual?

### A.3   Team maintenance

A successful leader understands that a team has its own personality, power, attitudes, standards and needs, and achieves success by taking this into account.

The key functions of the leader in meeting team needs are:

1   To set and maintain team objectives and team standards.
2   To involve the team as a whole in the achievement of objectives.
3   To maintain the unity of the team and to see that dissident activity is minimised.

*Checklist for team maintenance*

1   Do I set team objectives and make sure that everyone understands them?
2   Is the team clear as to the working standards expected from them? Am I fair and impartial in enforcing them? Is the team aware of the consequences of infringement?
3   Do I look for opportunities to build teamwork into jobs?
4   Do I take action on matters likely to disrupt the team?
5   Is there a formal, fair, and understood grievance procedure?
6   Do I welcome and encourage new ideas and suggestions from the team?
7   Do I provide regular opportunities for consultation before taking decisions affecting their work, plans, output, standards, etc.?
8   Do I regularly brief the group on the organisation's achievements, current plans and future developments?
9   Am I accurately reflecting the views and problems of the team to higher management?
10   Am I accurately reflecting company policy to the team and ensuring that they understand it?

## A.4   Summary

Your job as the leader is:

1   To get the required results.
2   To manage your interpersonal relationships and those within the team so that:
   (a)   The team works as a team.
   (b)   Each individual feels he is playing a vital part in the success of the team.

Your skill in achieving the required results through the group are matched by your skill in 'managing' the relationships of individuals with the team (see Table A.1). These are the functions of a leader — they are not inborn traits, but skills which you can recognise, practise and develop in order to become a better manager.

TABLE A.1

Managing people: management checklist

| Key functions | Task | Team | Individual needs |
|---|---|---|---|
| Define objective | Identify task and constraints | Set targets Involve team | Agree targets and responsibilities |
| Plan | Establish priorities Decide | Structure and delegate | Assess skills Train Delegate |
| Communicate | Brief and check understanding | Consult Obtain feedback | Listen Advise Enthuse |
| Support/control | Monitor progress Check standards | Co-ordinate Reconcile conflict | Recognise Encourage Counsel |
| Evaluate | Review Replan Summarise | Reward success Learn from failure | Appraise, guide and train |

# Summary:                                   Keys to Success

Looking back through all the headings in this book, we are reminded how diverse are the activities of the sales office. Running one effectively is far from easy. It may be useful to examine two final areas: *decision-making* and *the use of time*.

## Decision-making

As well as being diverse, the activities in the sales office are very numerous. Much of the manager's time is spent in making decisions — deciding between alternatives — many of them in themselves small, but all important to the operation with which he is engaged.

Whilst it may be true that there are no 'right' answers in business, the wrong decisions in any part of the operation can have a serious, sometimes crippling, effect. Experience is a vital factor in picking the best alternative, though too much reliance on it can create a false sense of security and stifle creativity, producing a sort of 'I've seen it all before' feeling.

A procedure that is logical and systematic and ensures due consideration of the alternatives, while not being infallible, will certainly help. The stages in such an approach can be viewed as follows:

### Step 1    Setting objectives

Before any action can be considered, the objectives of the exercise must be set. Unless you know where you are going, you cannot plan how to get there or how to measure your progress. For the objective to be valuable it must be as specific and as quantitative as possible. Goals such as 'increasing sales', 'improving customer service' and 'reducing costs' are useless, as they provide no basis for measurement. If the aim is to increase sales, it should be specified by how much and within what time period.

### Step 2    Evaluating the objective against other company objectives

When a clear, precise goal has been established, it should be compared with other company aims to ensure compatibility. Failure to do this is common, particularly in large companies.

This results in different sections of the firm working towards objectives which in themselves are reasonable but which when put together become mutually exclusive: for example, the sales office manager may be trying to maintain business with small accounts, whereas marketing or sales management are planning to service them exclusively via wholesalers.

*Step 3   Collecting information*

Information can now be collected from which plans can be developed. It is unwise to start this data collection stage until clear, compatible objectives have been defined, otherwise vast quantities of useless figures will be assembled 'for information' or 'in case we need them'. The hunger for information has been stimulated by the advance of research techniques and the progressive development of the computer. It is a great temptation to the manager to call for information simply because he knows it is available. Mountains of figures may give a sense of security, but information is costly to process and is only useful (and economic) when it contains answers to precise questions which have direct bearing on the decisions it is possible to take.

*Step 4   Analysing the information*

It is the objective which will guide the manager towards the questions to be answered and thus the information needed. The lines of analysis to be followed will in turn be indicated by such questions. For example, declining sales in one area of the country, perhaps owing to the larger customers buying from the competition, should not prompt us to ask for 'everything we know about the market'. What we really need is sales in that region broken down by customer type, possibly compared with similar figures for another area. From this analysis, we can proceed progressively through the relevant information, very much more precisely (and probably more quickly and economically) than starting with a dozen different breakdowns that attempt to show 'all about everything'.

*Step 5   Developing alternatives*

The whole basis of this method of approach is to encourage the manager to think more broadly and creatively about possible solutions to his problem. Sometimes, of course, the solution will become obvious from systematic processing of the data. In the majority of instances, however, no clear-cut answer will be found, a number of factors suggest themselves, or the answer lies in a combination of a number of factors.

*Step 6   Choosing 'the best' alternative*

This is the heart of the decision-making process. It is unlikely that all possible solutions can be implemented; one must be chosen. To help in this choice, consideration should be made of four criteria: cost, time, risk, and resources.

The costs of each alternative can be calculated and compared against the objective. Assuming that several approaches appear to be capable of achieving the objective, this might only narrow the choice. So the other yardsticks should also be used. Time taken might be a critical factor, or the element of risk (particularly of failure) or lack of certain resources might rule out other options: e.g. the critical staffing situation in many sales offices may preclude certain courses of action.

The choice of the 'best' alternative then is based on a consideration of all the advantages and disadvantages of all the possible alternatives. It is at this stage that experience can be particularly valuable. Its possible limiting effect will already have been overcome by the systematic search for alternatives.

Having made the choice, at least the manager will be well aware of what he had done in terms of the possible drawbacks of his decision and the discarded alternatives. It will also be easier at some time in the future to look back and assess why such a decision was, in fact, made.

## Step 7    Communicating the decision

This is a step too often omitted. And yet unless all concerned know what is being done, impact will be lost. It is commonplace to find inside sales staff whose first knowledge of an advertising campaign is gained from customers. The communication must be systematically planned. Information may well have to be passed by different methods and in different forms to different people, in writing, by telephone, meetings etc. By communicating only necessary information by the most appropriate methods, far better results will be gained than by a blanket memorandum with copies to everybody.

## Step 8    Setting up the control system

Remember that this stage occurs before implementation. This is because in many cases the process of implementing a plan destroys the ability to evaluate it. For example, in a situation where it is believed that inside sales staff lack product knowledge, the decision might be taken to run a training programme. At the end of the course a test is given in which the average score is 90 per cent. It might be concluded, therefore, that the programme was successful. But, as there has been no measurement of what the test score would have been at the beginning of the programme, it can never then be known whether it was successful or not.

## Step 9    Implementing the decision

Putting the decision into action should now be easy. It will have been clearly stated what is to be done towards what objective and why that particular action has been chosen, all concerned will have been informed, and the system of evaluation will have been set. Research has shown that if change is to be implemented, then specific tasks should be allocated to particular people and deadlines laid down for the tasks to be completed. Vague requests for action some time will inevitably result in failure.

## Step 10    Evaluating the decision

Again assuming quantitative objectives, clear decisions and predefined control systems, evaluation is simple. The problems of control and evaluation in management are caused by lack of clear yardsticks against which to compare. If the manager simply sets broad qualitative goals of increasing sales 'as much as possible' or improving customer service, he will have the utmost difficulty in evaluating the results. There will usually be no common definition of what constitutes an increase or an improvement.

Figure S.1 shows in summary form the decision-making steps, the key points to check at each step and an example of a decision taken by this method, relating to increasingly direct telephone sales from the office.

134

| STEPS | CHECK | EXAMPLE |
|---|---|---|
| 1 Setting objectives | Are they specific and quantitative? | To increase direct telephone sales revenue by 10 per cent in next six months compared with same period last year. To increase customers to 500. To hold sales costs at same level as last year |
| 2 Evaluating the objectives | Do they conflict with other goals? | Production is available, also promotional help |
| 3 Collecting the information | Have the questions to be answered been clearly defined? | Need last year's sales broken down by customer, product and telesales operator. Also market research data on potential available and competitive activity |
| 4 Analysing the information | Is it known what is being seached for? | Specific questions to be answered include: Can current customers buy more? How many prospects are there? What is current sales force call rate? What is order: call ratio? |
| 5 Developing alternatives | Have all possibilities been listed? | (Assuming above work done) (a) Increase call frequency on customers (b) Increase prospecting rate (c) Improve selling skills by training |
| 6 Choosing the 'best' alternative | Have all alternatives been evaluated in terms of cost, time, risk and resources? | (a) Cost increase because need more operations. Delay in recruiting. Risk in taking on more new men. Personnel dept resources involved. Employment Legislation considerations. (b) No cost — can do with existing team. Some time to reorganise. Low risk. Low resource use (c) Cost of training. Time for training. Experience elsewhere shows training effective therefore risk low. No resources, can use consultants. Choose (c) as likely to be most effective though not cheapest |
| 7 Communicating the decision | Have the right people been told the appropriate information by the appropriate methods? | Advise marketing director by memo. Brief inside sales team meeting. Give terms of reference to consultants at meeting |
| 8 Setting up the control system | What will be measured, how and when? | Best yardsticks of increased effectiveness are order: call ratio and average order size. Monitor now before action starts |

**Fig. S.1 Ten-step decision-making. (Adapted from decision-making chart in M.T. Wilson's *Managing a Sales Force*)**

| STEPS | CHECK | EXAMPLE |
|---|---|---|
| 9 Implementing the decision | Have specific tasks been allo-cated with specific timings? | Run training programme. Revise sales targets. Concentrate on lists of customers with further potential |
| 10 Evaluating the decision | Has the decision been evaluated against the objectives? | Appraisal of training pro-gramme. Actuals *v* targets on monthly basis |

Fig. S. 1 Ten-step decision-making (cont.)

### The use of time

Quite simply, management takes time. In a job where much of the manager's time goes on his share of the activity this needs remembering. For example, we must expect to have problems with the motivation of our team if we never do anything about it. Further, we cannot expect that if we find half an hour haphazardly every week or fortnight for 'a quick bit of motivation', all will be well. We have to set time aside consciously for review and action in many such areas if we are to have any chance of balancing the situation and being an effective manager.

As was said at the beginning of this section, running an effective sales office is far from easy. Let us conclude by reviewing the mix of characteristics and considerations that make success more likely.

It is not enough to be a *good administrator* — though without the sorting-out of priorities, without smooth handling of enquiries, files, paperwork, correspondence and records, a sales office will never be effective.

It is not enough to be a *good salesman* — though it is essential to have an understanding and familiarity with sales techniques, be able to recognise sales opportunities, and ensure both we and members of our team meet them.

It is not enough to be an *effective man-manager* — though it is vital to be able to lead and motivate a close-knit and enthusiastic team, tackling a diverse range of activity in hectic conditions.

*We have to understand and pass on an understanding of the role* of the sales office, seeing it as a vital tactical weapon in the marketing operation. This means that we must have an appreciation of what marketing is, and of the various ways in which, directly or indirectly, the sales office can contribute to company profits.

A prerequisite for contributing effectively is for the sales office manager to be able to *identify priorities*. With such a variety of activities, with incoming calls and enquiries so unpredictable, the manager either adheres to rigid sets of rules, and runs an adequate office, or has the skill and initiative to recognise different priorities and to get the best out of them, so building up a really effective operation.

Identifying priorities is of little use, however, unless the manager is able to *organise* the sales office to deal with them. This calls for abilities in managing and controlling time, systems and men.

To be effective means being a consistent, sales-oriented man-manager, able to accept ideas from others and to cope with the problems of the urgent as well as the important.

A final checklist (Figure S.2) is intended to help measure progress towards your goal.

## ARE YOU A FULLY COMPETENT SALES OFFICE MANAGER?

Rate your knowledge and skill in each area

1  Highly knowledgeable and skilled — no further training needed at the moment

2  Above average — could benefit from further development but not urgent

3  Below average — need deep training which should be arranged soon

4  Low-need training immediately. Dangerous to take decisions in these areas without consultation

Better still, ask your superior to rate you

|  | 1 | 2 | 3 | 4 | Action |
|---|---|---|---|---|---|
| 1 Knowledge of context in which we operate<br>(a) company organisation<br>(b) market characteristics<br>(c) sales process and marketing function |  |  |  |  |  |
| 2 Managing the activity knowledge and skill<br>(a) setting up the organisation<br>(b) managing time<br>(c) managing systems<br>(d) controlling |  |  |  |  |  |
| 3 Sales knowledge and skill<br>(a) product knowledge (customer orientated)<br>(b) company knowledge (jargon-free)<br>(c) sales technique —<br>☐ telephone<br>☐ written<br>☐ face to face |  |  |  |  |  |
| 4 Man-management knowledge and skill<br>(a) development and appraisal<br>(b) delegating<br>(c) leadership<br>(d) motivation<br>(e) decision-making |  |  |  |  |  |

**Fig. S.2  Knowledge and skills checklist**

# *Further Reading*

Everyone in the sales office tends always to be under pressure and cannot readily find time for intensive reading. The following list has therefore been kept short, and includes a number of 'booklets' and other references rather than just textbooks.

## *General*

*Choosing and using Charts*, Video Arts
Moore, C., *How To Handle Customer Complaints*, Gower Press
Roman, Eva, *The Art of Dictation*, Gower Press
*What is a Computer?*, Video Arts

## *Man management/leadership*

Adair, John, *Training for Leadership*, Gower Press
Adair, John, *Decisions Decisions*, Video Arts
Drucker, Peter, *The Practice of Management*, Pan Books
Herzberg, F., *Work and the Nature of Man*, Staples Press
*How Am I Doing?* (appraisal interview), Video Arts
*I'd Like a Word With You* (The discipline interview), Video Arts
Lidstone, John, *Motivating Your Sales Force*, Gower Press
Lidstone, John, *Recruiting and Selecting Successful Salesmen*, Gower Press

## *Marketing*

Morse, S., *The Practical Approach to Marketing Management*, McGraw-Hill
Wilson, M.T., *The Management of Marketing*, Gower

*Selling and sales techniques*

Gillam, A., *Commercial Salesmanship*, UKCTA
Lidstone, J., *Negotiating Profitable Sales*, Gower Press
Tietjen, T., *Telephone Techniques*, Video Arts

*Systems*

Lund, P.R., *Sales Reports Records and Systems*, Gower Press
Paulden, S., *How to Deliver on Time*, Gower Press

# Index

Adair, John,
    *Training for Leadership*, 127
Advertising, 9
Appraisal, staff, 109
    meetings, 110–113
Assessment, staff, 109

Birds Eye Co., 103
Buying process, 54

Capital, 5
Charts,
    bar, 45–46
    pie, 46
    time, 48
Chesterton, G.K., 33
Coca Cola Co., 103
Company, the,
    functions of, 5
    image, 61–70
    need for growth, 11–12
    need for profit, 11
    resources, 5
Complaints, 74
    as originators of sales, 93
    dealing with, 76–77
    forms, 74–75
    meaning of, 74
Control, sales force,
    items needing control, 39
    standards, 39–40

Correspondence,
    and company image, 67–69
    customers' as originators of sales, 93
Customer, 10, 57
    needs of, 10–11, 57
    sales office services for, 20

Decision-making, 136–140
Delegation, 115–118
    benefits, 115–116
    evaluating results of, 117–118
    monitoring, 116–117
    reducing risks of, 116–117
Development, staff, 109, 114
Discount calculator, 44–45
Distribution, 9

Enquiries,
    as originators of sales, 93
Environment,
    and marketing, 7
*Evening News*, 103
*Evening Standard*, 103

Filing, 37–38
    how to file, 37–38
    what to file, 37
Forms,
    assessment, 109
    complaint, 74–75
    design of, 44
    enquiry, 72–73

Graphs,
  direct proportion, 48
  use of, 45

Herzberg, Frederick, 120
  *Work and the Nature of Man*, 120
Histograms, 47

Image, company, 61
  improving the, 62
  influences on, 61, 62–70
Information presentation, 44–48
  use of illustrations, 44, 48
Information storage, 34
  continuing to keep 'one-off' information, 36
  duplication, 35
  electronic, 34–35
  filing, 37–38
Initiated activities, 92–95
  kinds of, 93–95

Jargon, 60
Job descriptions, 22, 25, 111

Labour, 5
Leadership, 128–131
  achieving the task, 129
  meeting individual needs, 129–130
  team maintenance, 130
Lidstone, John,
  *Recruiting and Selecting Successful Salesmen*, 103
  *Motivating Your Sales Force*, 119

Market, 4
  segments, 4–5
Market research, 4, 9
Marketing, 3–4, 16
  defined, 4
  environment and, 7
  mix, 5
  part of company 'strategy', 8
  system, 4–8
Marketing Improvements,
  survey of telephone selling, 103
Motivation, staff, 119–127
  achievement, 123
  advancement, 125
  aspects of, 120
  dissatisfaction with company policy and administration, 120
  dissatisfaction with supervision, 120
  dissatisfiers, 120–123
  interpersonal relations, 121

  job environment, 120, 121
  job itself, 120, 124
  motivators, 120, 123–125
  recognition, 123–124
  responsibility, 124–125
  salary, 123
  security, 122–123
  status, 122

New applications,
  as originators of sales, 93

Operating manual, 20–29
  as reference, 22
  contents, 22–23
Orders,
  as originators of fresh sales, 93

Product,
  benefits, 56–57, 80
  development, 9
  feature/benefit analysis, 57–58
  features, 58, 59, 82
Priorities, 30–31
Promotion, 9

Reception,
  and company image, 64
Receptionist, 64
Response activities, sales office, 71–91
  dealing with complaints, 76–77
  need for accuracy, 72
  need for awareness of time, 72–74
  sales letters, 77–87
  telephone selling, 87–91
  timing, 72

Sales, 9
  direct, 20
  of consumer goods via retailers, 13
  of repeat-purchases, 12–13
  selling benefits, 56–57, 59–60, 89
  selling sequence, 53–55
  using product information effectively, 55
Sales force, 15
  control of, 39
  cost of, 16, 103
  liaison with sales office, 97
  representatives' reports as originators of sales, 93
  role of, 96–97
  sales office services for, 20

Sales letters, 77–80
    body of, 83
    ending of, 83–84
    importance of first sentence, 81
    language, 84
    opening of, 81–83
    persuasive, 80
    successful, 80–81
    words and expressions to avoid, 84–87
Sales management, 15, 49
    by exception, 49
    controlling sales force, 39
    sales office services for, 20
    use of time, 136
Sales office, 8, 16
    activities, 19–20
    advantages over sales force, 16
    and marketing cycle, 9–10
    areas of direct effect on sales, 53
    briefing switchboard, 63
    collecting information for control, 40
    dangers in becoming admin. wing only, 92
    direct link with customers, 10, 13
    general administration, 20
    importance of follow-ups, 15
    importance of service to customer, 11, 16
    influence on company growth, 12
    influence on company profit, 12
    liaison with sales force, 97
    making best use of time, 32–33
    monitoring information for control, 41–43
    need for continuous manning, 66
    opportunities to initiate business, 92
    order fulfilment, 20
    presenting information for control, 44–48
    role in 'multi-stage' selling, 13–14
    sales process and, 12–13
    setting priorities, 30–32, 33
    staff attitudes and company image, 64–66
    supporting role in controlling sales force, 39, 49, 53, 96
    'tactical weapon' in marketing, 7, 8
Scheduling, 31–32
Service to customers, 11, 16
Standards, control, 39–40
    absolute, 40
    diagnostic, 40
    moving, 40
    variance from, 39, 49
Support activities, 96–102
    conscious alternatives for low-priority prospects, 101–102
    gaining information, 100

making appointments for salesmen, 98–99
    provision of information, 97–98
    selecting information, 100–101
Switchboard, telephone, 62–63

Telephone,
    message pads, 63, 72
    selling by, 87–91
Telephone selling, 103–106
    advantages, 87, 103–104
    criteria for success, 104
    limitations, 87
    need to plan, 87–88
    questioning method, 89
    sales hints, 91
    statement method, 89
    steps in adoption of, 104–106
    technique, 88–90
    winding up, 90
Telephone switchboard,
    and company image, 62–63
Time management, 32–33
Training, staff, 113–114
    formal, 113
    informal, 113

Wrigley Co., 103